The
Underground Guide
to

– 2nd edition –

- Also from Manic D Press -

The Underground Guide to Los Angeles, 2nd edition
Pleasant Gehman, editor

The Sofa Surfing Handbook:
a guide for modern nomads
Juliette Torrez, editor

The
Underground Guide
to

SAN FRANCISCO

– 2nd edition –

Jennifer Joseph
editor

Manic D Press
San Francisco

Dedicated to
the non-stop amazingness that keeps us here

Thanks to the contributors, and to the Manic D production team: Wendy Yee, Yolanda Montijo, Lori Noll, Sarah Trott, Gloria Smith.

drawings: Isabel Samaras   cover: Scott Idleman / BLINK

ISBN 0-916397-69-6

ISSN 1542-0841

CONTENTS

FOREWARD!

San Francisco is the greatest city on the planet, right? It's been through cataclysmic changes over the years but that's just how San Francisco is, ever since the Gold Rush days. It's an amazing place to visit and an even better place to live.

Okay, now that we all agree, let's just say that this book is completely eclectic, outrageously opinionated, and was created with both visitor and resident in mind. I doubt that anyone who reads this will be like, "Yawn, same old tired tour book stuff..."

I know there are things in here that few people know about, and besides it's a handy reference guide for living that ever-elusive affordable lifestyle here in America's most breathtaking city. It's the book I wish I had when I first moved here...

Enjoy—

Jen.

Jennifer Joseph

P.S. Do yourself a favor and buy a MUNI map, available at most corner stores. This map shows all bus lines, streetcars, cable cars, and more. Please note telephone area codes: 415 for SF, 510 for Berkeley and Oakland. Have fun!

JEN'S TOP 10 TIPS
FOR CHEAP & EASY SF LIVING
(IN NO PARTICULAR ORDER)

1. **The SF Public Library**. With more than a dozen branches in neighborhoods throughout the city, the SFPL offers free internet access and borrowing privileges for books, magazines, DVDs, videotapes, CDs, and more. Free programs for kids and adults happen often - The Library rules! It's free! It's amazing! Just return that borrowed stuff on time OR ELSE! Don't be a loser!

2. **SF Rec & Parks**. Play tennis, play golf, go swimming for little or no money, thanks to those nice folks at Rec & Parks. Swimming pools are located throughout the city and offer free swim classes, as well as water aerobics and more. Tennis courts exist in many neighborhoods; golf is in Golden Gate and McLaren Parks. Year-round free programs for kids are sponsored throughout town by Rec & Parks, too. Look in the phonebook's SF government pages under Rec & Parks.

3. **Community Gardens**. Just because you live in the city doesn't mean you can't grow your own tomatoes. **San Francisco League of Urban Gardeners** (SLUG) sponsors community gardens throughout the city, call them for a current list. Some may have waiting lists, others will have openings.

4. **Fresh produce markets**. Whether you shop on Stockton Street in Chinatown, Clement Street in the Richmond, or on Mission Street, there are real deals to be found when it comes to fruits and vegetables: four avocados for $1?! You betcha. If you're motivated, the Alemany Farmers Market at the foot of Bernal Heights RULES! It doesn't get any fresher, and rarely gets any cheaper.

5. **Volunteer**. Tickets too expensive? Be an usher at the Fillmore, the Ballet, the Opera, or any theater. Offer to help at Burning Man, Bay to Breakers, or any other cost-prohibitive activity you want to do. People are needed to make all this stuff happen, and sometimes it's more fun to part of it than just a spectator.

6. The **Museum of Modern Art** is free everyday it's open for the last 45 minutes till closing -- plenty of time to catch that new exhibit. Your library card gets you in free to the **Yerba Buena Art Galleries** across the street.

7. **City College**. Take that ceramics class you've always wanted, or Beginning Italian, or one of about a zillion other offerings for less than you'd spend for a ticket to see someone lame at the Shoreline Amphitheater.

8. **Oakland A's Baseball**. Wednesdays are dollar days: $1 admission and $1 hot dogs. Go A's! (The Giants offer free ballfield-level views from the bay side of Pac Bell Park.)

9. **Ocean Beach**. Oh yeah, the Pacific Ocean is right here. Take a long walk and get some fresh air. Find a sand dollar. Watch the sunset. Feel better about everything. **Golden Gate Park** is also an urban oasis. Look for the monkey puzzle trees, they're awesome!

10. **Burritos!** These will keep you alive no matter what: rice, beans, salsa, and more for under $5. Recommended purveyors: Taqueria Cancun, Pancho Villa, El Toro.

COMING & GOING

Cheap Airline Tickets • San Francisco's free weekly newspapers have advertisements for cheap travel agencies, as does the Sunday *Chronicle*'s Travel section. **JetBlue Airways** (800-538-2583) often has the cheapest one-way and roundtrip flights into and out of Oakland. **Southwest Airlines** (800-435-9792) occasionally offers a 2-for-1 deal anywhere they fly or $99 coast-to-coast one way, depending on the season. **United** (800-241-6522) and **Alaska Airlines** (800-426-0333) sometimes have 2-for-1 deals to Portland, Seattle, or Los Angeles. For online cheap tickets, check out hotwire.com, lowestfare.com, cheaptickets.com, or orbitz.com. For student fares, use STA.com. Regardless of airline, it's often cheaper to fly out of or into Oakland Airport, so check availability and prices. Always check the airlines' websites for best prices - best time to check prices by phone is just after midnight since reservations that are not paid for expire at midnight so cheap seats might be available.

Getting To & From the Airports

SFO • Cheap and reliable if you don't have much baggage is the **SamTrans** bus #292 or KX (800-660-4287). Runs often during the day, less frequently at night. Goes to and from the Transbay Terminal downtown at First & Mission Streets. Catch local **MUNI** (673-6864) buses to & from there. BART (510-465-2278) will soon go to SFO . Shuttle vans are available to and from the airport. **Supershuttle** (558-8500) is a fairly reliable company. Taxis cost upwards of $25 dollars but up to five people can ride for one fare so it could be really cheap for a group of more than two.

Oakland • Take the **BART** (510-465-2278) train. A little more than an hour to SF. Inexpensive. SF BART has a service called AirBart which runs every 10 minutes from the Coliseum to the Oakland terminal for $2. Information can be obtained at (989-2278).

Other Travel Concepts

Bus • **Greyhound** (800-231-2222) gives 15% discounts to students with Student Advantage Cards, which can be obtained online for free. It comes and goes. So does the hound alternative, **Green Tortoise** (494 Broadway at Kearny, 956-7500): call them for more info.

Train • Ride the rails with **Amtrak** (800-872-7245).

Driveaway Cars • If you have some time and a clean driving record, driveaway cars can be a cheap and fun way to get around the country. Check with **Auto Driveaway Co.** in San Jose (408-984-4999) for car availability and destinations.

COUCHSURFING ALTERNATIVES

Unless you have some pals in town, you're going to need someplace to crash. Even if you have pals in town, chances are there's already someone sleeping on the sofa.

Just Passing Thru • **AYH/Hosteling International** operates 2 hostels in SF, a large one (266 beds) downtown (312 Mason at Geary, 788-5604) and a small one (172 beds) at Ft. Mason (Bay at Franklin, Bldg. 240, 771-7277). They're clean, safe, and cheap but have rules and offer little privacy. The **Green Tortoise Guest Hous**e (494 Broadway at Kearny, 834-1000) has private rooms for $48 and shared rooms for $38, breakfast and internet access are included. Their 39 rooms are often booked up two weeks in advance so reservations are definitely recommended. Other hostels exist on Folsom between 7th & 8th Sts. **Easy Going Guest House** has two hipster locations (1104 Harrison at 7th St.; 3147 Mission near Army, 401-6100), dorm beds $18 and up, private rooms $40 and up, reservations recommended during the summer. For a righteous mini-vacation, ride a bicycle or the 76 MUNI bus (weekends only) out to the **Marin Headlands** (104 beds, 4 family rooms) hostel (941 Fort Barry, Sausalito, 331-2777) and spend the night. Fast and easy urban escape!

Residential Hotels • Rent by the day, week, or month. Shared bathrooms usually. Run the gamut from decent to frightful. Other neighborhoods besides the Tenderloin featuring these low-cost accommodations include North Beach (**Europa**, 310 Columbus at Broadway, 391-5779; **Golden Eagle**, 402 Broadway at Montgomery, 781-6859) and South-of-Market.

Longterm Shelter • So you've decided to stay for awhile. For shared housing, check the ubiquitous bulletin board at **Rainbow Grocery** (1745 Folsom at 14th St., 863-0620). The free weekly papers also have listings, as does **www.craigslist.com**. The best way to find your own apartment is to pick your desired neighborhood and look for 'For Rent' signs. Perseverance is key. Have cash ready for a deposit (usually first and last months, and a 'cleaning' deposit, usually equal to one month's rent). Once you get your name on a lease, hang out for a while: rent control currently limits rent increases to less than 3% per year, and landlords must pay interest annually on your security deposit. If you have questions about rent control or experience landlord problems, call the **SF Rent Board** (252-4602). If you move to a neighborhood that requires a parking permit to park your vehicle on the street for more than two hours, call the **Department of Parking & Traffic** (554-5000). Get one ASAP to avoid tickets or worse. Temporary permits are available if you're expecting visitors.

Where To Put Parents for Under $70 • My parents often don't appreciate my standard of living, though they're certainly grateful that I don't live with them anymore, and believe me, the feeling's extremely mutual. However, when they inevitably come to town, it's unlikely that they'll be making couch reservations, so here are a few non-motel alternatives. **Metro Hotel** (319 Divisadero at Oak, 861-5364) near the Haight has rooms with private baths, $66 and up. **Grant Plaza Hotel** (465 Grant at Pine, 800-472-6899) is on the edge of Chinatown near Union Square, rooms start around $60. The charming **San Remo Hotel** (2237 Mason at Chestnut, 776-8688) near Fisherman's Wharf has rooms from around $55 with shared bath. Bed-and-breakfasts are a great way to go - it's usually someone renting out a spare room in their house or a separate in-law apartment. Make reservations through **Bed & Breakfast San Francisco** (899-0060, www.bbsf.com).

The Hippest Hotels In S.F. • Here are a few joints that have distinguished themselves for whatever reasons. The **Phoenix Hotel** (601 Eddy at Larkin, 776-1380) is where all the up-and-coming rock bands (like Dogstar, Green Day, and everybody else on MTV) stay when they're in town. Rooms start at $129, and this is also the location of that ever-trendy restaurant, **Backflip**, where you can have dinner next to Keanu Reeves. Another swell joint is the **Triton Hotel** (324 Grant at Sutter, 394-0500), which is decorated in ultra-modern art deco furniture, special rates start at $105. The recently opened **Hotel Del Sol** (3100 Webster at Greenwich, 921-5520) is fun and located in the Marina, not far from North Beach and the Wharf.

HOW TO FIND A RENTAL
BEFORE WE WASH OFF INTO THE BAY
BY STACEY LEWIS

So, you want to live in San Francisco? Let me tell you my secrets… My recent forays into the rental rat race started the day our landlord graciously allowed me to co-sign a lease with my roommates. He then gently announced that his ex-wife/co-owner of the property, was thinking of moving in at the end of the year. "Heeeeeeeeere's Johnny!" pounded through my own door, threatening the much talked about "owner-move-in" eviction. (Owner-move-ins, the taking over of a property by the landlord or their relative, is the top strategy used by landlords to evict tenants, according to San Francisco's Rent Board.)

After ignoring the problem for a couple of days, I jumped on it. For two months I thoroughly investigated the many rental resources SF has to offer as well as using the *SF Chronicle* Real Estate section. To leap to the end of the story, my bestest friends and I did eventually land a beautiful, rent-controlled apartment in the outer Mission - wood floors, working fireplace, deck - so there is hope!

Initially, I signed up with a rental agency: **Rent Tech** (4054 18th St. at Hartford, 863-7368, www.renttech.com). The not-cheap $100 membership fee buys you 90 days of rental listings, which are emailed or faxed daily. At their office, free use of their phones to call landlords, computer access, and decent coffee are offered to ease your ordeal. They also supply an excellent map of the city, which lists even the most obscure streets and clearly demarcates neighborhoods. Plan on providing a general profile of the home you're looking for including the number of bedrooms, the minimum and maximum amount of money you're willing to spend, desired neighborhoods, and for many of us the big factor: do they accept pets or more specifically, cats and dogs?

There are some good strategies to use when setting up your renter profile. You're allowed to change your preferences, including how much money you're willing to pay. The folks at Rent Tech get very amused by phone calls scrambling around with numbers. I also asked them to remove my "cat allowed" request when I quickly realized that there are twice as many landlords preferring renters who don't have pets (why I oughtta…). If you have the option of moving into a place you really like and they don't accept pets, consider sneaking Fluffy, Woody, and Lolita in with discretion.

An obvious thing to consider when checking out apartments and flats is the number of rooms that might accommodate you and your roommates. For instance, we looked at some 2-bedroom apartments to see if a common room or dining room could be converted into a third bedroom. Most often this was not possible, but it's worth exploring. Most landlords count bathrooms as part of the total number of rooms so be sure to note this when looking at listings.

Get a rental application, available from any rental broker, and be ready to deal with the dreaded credit check. You'll have to lay out an extra $30-$50 to each landlord for a credit check, which they may or may not want to do on their own. Agencies like Rent Tech provide this service for $35 and will generate sealed credit checks for you to give to landlords, but I found it a waste of money as our landlord had his own way of doing things. If you think you have bad credit, definitely get a look at your credit history before sharing this information with a landlord. If, for example, you have many student loans but now work full-time, your report may show lack of or negative credit. Be straightforward with your prospective landlord as they'll appreciate your honesty. And remember that they wouldn't go to the trouble of a credit check if they didn't like you in the first place. Also, if your finances are shaky or you're still a student, ask your folks to co-sign a lease. Landlords are very open to this. And tell them that paying rent is your first priority; that in fact you'd rather starve than have them miss out on their tenement dues.

When showing up for appointments to look at homes, make sure you're early and dare I say it, shower, shave, and iron those clothes! Most impressive to a landlord, I think, is to hand them a prepared rental application and sealed credit checks for yourself and your roommates at the showings. Do mention that you like the house and especially the neighborhood. If public transportation is close by and you use it, let the landlords know. Once they can get a picture of you living in the 'hood, you've got them hooked.

Truth be told, we found our place through the newspaper, the most unreliable source of information according to many people. (And I should mention that we received a partial refund from Rent Tech as we didn't successfully use them to find our home - one of the finer fine points of their company policy.) The Sunday edition of the *Chronicle* with the Real Estate section comes out Friday evening, so you can begin your Saturday mornings with a latte and a good look up and down the columns. Keep careful records of the places you call as it gets confusing. Be prepared for a phone interview, an initial screening.

It's important to give yourself as many options for finding homes as possible, through agencies, newspapers, and other sources, some listed below. Tell friends and acquaintances you're looking for a place. Post a notice at work. Instead of emailing annoying spam to your buddies, let them know what's up. Make them feel sorry for you. Get them to feed you, love you, and give up their own homes. There are options, many, many options. I have faith that you will find an abode here. If not, there's always... Oakland.

Housing Resources

***Craig's list**: www.craigslist.org (free housing listings)
***Rent Tech**: www.renttech.com 863-7368 (roommate services, too)
***San Francisco For Rent**: sf4rent.com 440-7368
***Want Ads**: www.sfgate.com

HOUSING HELL
BY JAMES TRACY

San Francisco has always been a city of refuge whether it be for families fleeing death squads in Central America, queers running from homophobic families, blacks migrating for better jobs, Asians building so much of our city, or Irish and other Europeans looking for a kinder life. San Francisco has been here for everyone, arms open wider than other cities at times. Writers, artists, and performers have created a cultural life unparalleled elsewhere. Activists have continuously reshaped local politics. San Francisco has always been a city of change, the only constant around here is change.

For rich and poor alike, a good social network opens up doors. Get involved with community groups and you'll meet folks. Put news of your plight out - you'll find people are willing to help.

Keeping Your Housing A lot of tenants think that they have no protection under law and move out the minute a landlord tells them to. You have legal rights, however scarce. Use them!

When you rent an apartment, you basically control it until you give it up or a landlord gets the court to agree to throw you out. Evictions happen only in court. This means that no one can throw you out except the Sheriff AFTER you have lost a court case. The police can't throw you out, your property manager can't either.

If your landlord or anyone working for him throws your belonging into the streets they are breaking California Civil Code Section 789.3 and the landlord is liable for $100 a day in penalties.

Get some help! The tenants organizations listed below assist thousands of tenants a year, meaning that they can help you build a strategy to stay in your home since they know from experience what has worked and what hasn't.

The Eviction Notice According to the SF Tenants Union handbook, "All evictions begin with a three or thirty day notice. You do not have to leave your home by the end of this notice and your landlord can't force you out. If you haven't moved by the end of this period, only then can the landlord can begin the legal eviction process."

In San Francisco, landlords have a whopping fourteen "just causes" to remove you with. The eviction notice must state what cause the landlord has. If the landlord forgot to write down why they are doing the eviction you can have the proceedings thrown out in court. There are other technicalities that can forestall an eviction. Talk to a tenant counselor about these.

The "Unlawful Detainer" Lawsuit, The Summons & Complaint If you wake up one morning and find a piece of paper that reads UNLAWFUL DETAINER/SUMMONS AND COMPLAINT nailed to your door; you know your landlord is getting serious. You MUST respond to this in five days or the court will automatically rule against you, no matter how good your defense is. Begin counting the five days the day after you receive the Summons; weekends and holidays count as days, but the five days cannot end on a weekend or holiday.

The Answer Respond to the Summons by completing a court form called an "Answer." Some tenants have made the mistake of thinking that a handwritten note will do! NO! For about thirty dollars you can have a paralegal write your answer out in the proper, legal, typewritten form.

Going To Court The judge will try to convince you to settle with the landlord before the trial actually begins, usually at a settlement conference in his or her chambers. If you don't like what's being offered, you have the right to take it to a trial. The jury pool is likely to have a large number of renters on it, which works in your favor. However, folks who lose their proceeding sometimes have to pay the legal costs of the landlord and have their credit records damaged. Once again having a good legal strategy worked out with tenant counselors or lawyers can help you weigh the risks.

The Sheriff Once the Sheriff has received the court order, he will come and post a Notice To Vacate on your door. Sheriffs in SF only evict on Wednesdays. During the Great Depression in the 1930s neighbors used to physically resist "Eviction Wednesdays" to defend their neighborhood from displacement. Oh, for the good old days.

If you can't leave within the five days, you can go back to court and file a "Stay of Execution." You will need to pay one week's rent to the court and this will delay the eviction for another week.

A Word on Roommates The number two cause of displacement, right after capitalism, is dysfunctional roommate relationships. As long as you're not in danger of great bodily harm, try mediation. It's a lot easier to hold onto your housing than look for a new place to live which will mean a rent increase for sure. Community Boards (920-3820) has free arbitration services.

Organizing The rights that you have as a renter came because folks organized politically to get them. Still so many tenants just accept as inevitable that they will have to leave; that gentrification is inevitable and that we might as well roll over and die. This is only as true as long as people stay unorganized and uninvolved. In San Francisco where every second person identifies as an "activist" it's funny how many people will run off to the next World Trade Organization conference but not lift a finger when low-income housing in their own city is systematically destroyed. Go figure. Here are some suggestions:

Join a tenant organization such as the **Housing Rights Committee** or the **SF Tenants Union**. You'll be kept up-to date about important actions, protests and events. The landlords in SF are especially organized (since most of them don't have real jobs) and can pack Supervisors' chambers by the hundreds.

Organize a tenants association in your building or neighborhood. Talk to your neighbors so that your landlord can't pit you against each other. Find out about who is getting evicted on your block and why. Then do something about it! Some folks I know in SF have posted trilingual signs that read "This is an Eviction Free Zone: Any Attempts at Eviction Will Be Fought Against," and the landlord has not been able to sell the building for a year!

Don't forget the art of direct action! Some of the most successful eviction defense efforts have happened when folks have picketed, carried on rent strikes, committed civil disobedience, etc. Even though you have certain legal rights, the sheer amount of evictions proves the point that "the system" favors the property owner instead of the tenant.

Tenants Rights Resources:

Housing Rights Committee of SF: 703-8644

SF Tenants Union: 282-5525

St. Peter's Housing Committee: 487-9203

Coalition on Homelessness: 346-3740

Oakland/East Bay Eviction Defense Collaborative: 510-452-4541

SF Rent Board: 252-4602

EMPLOYMENT IDEAS

Right now, there *are* jobs in the Bay Area but most of them are low-paying service jobs, e.g. restaurant, retail, or basic office work. It's really hard to make ends meet nowadays on less than $10/hour.

Non-permanent Employment • Get one outfit that consists of a dark skirt or trousers and a light-colored button-down shirt. Walk into any temp agency listed under 'Employment' in the yellow pages and tell them you just moved here and were a (choose one or all): a. file clerk; b. receptionist; c. secretary; in your former hometown. Make up a list of where you worked and for how long before you go in (they won't call long distance to check). To be a receptionist, all you have to know is how to answer a phone. To be a file clerk, you have to know the alphabet. Once you're signed up with several temp agencies, call them relentlessly. Do take the first job they offer you, so they know you're serious about working. Even if it's picking fleas off corporate chimps. Temp agencies pay weekly.

Apply the above general concept to restaurant work, except make up a history of being a: a. busperson; b. waitron; c. cook. Do not stop by during lunch or dinner hours. Tips=cash. No waiting for a paycheck.

If all else fails, you can always find employment in one of San Francisco's foremost time-honored occupations, the bike messenger. Think about it. You get to be outdoors all day, take breaks whenever you want. No bosses breathing down your neck. Even if you don't want to pedal, you could always be a dispatcher. Check the yellow pages under 'Delivery Service'.

Long Term Employment • Most public libraries have computers with internet access that anyone can use for free, so go to the nearest library and check out www.hotjobs.com for hundreds of listings in every kind of employment. Another way is to figure out where you'd like to work (The Museum of Modern Art? UCSF? Your favorite radio station?), look up their number in the phone book, and ask for Human Resources when you call. Ask if there are any job openings, you might be surprised - some of the best places to work never advertise. Here are a few more resources that may be worth checking out:

Online, there's **Craig's List** (www.craigslist.org), an online community with a variety of good local listings. The free Jobs & Careers Center at the **Main Library** (100 Larkin at Grove, 557-4400) is open everyday and provides lots of info on resume writing etc. as well as current job listings for dozens of Bay Area companies, as well as newspapers and magazines with tons of listings. **Experience Unlimited**

(745 Franklin at Turk, 771-1776) a.k.a. Job Club is a service of the State of California Employment Development Department which helps people find jobs. **Media Alliance** (814 Mission at 4th St., 546-6334) has a jobfile hotline for art, writing, publishing, video, film, etc. gigs. Media Alliance members are also eligible for group medical and dental insurance (what a concept!). There's a newsletter called *Opportunity NOCs* which lists job offerings at non-profit organizations. It's available at **The Foundation Center** (312 Sutter at Grant, 397-0902), a good place to do research if you're looking for free money for your project (whatever that project may be).

EMERGENCY INFORMATION

Dial 911 from any telephone for police, fire department, or an ambulance.

24-Hour Suicide Prevention Hotline: 781-0500

24-Hour Domestic Violence Hotline: 800-540-5433

Trauma Recovery and Rape Treatment Center: 821-3222 (8am-5pm M-F)

SF Women Against Rape: 647-7273 (24 Hours)

24-Hour Pharmacy: **Walgreen's** (498 Castro at 18th St., 861-6276. 3136 Divisadero at Lombard; 931-6417)

24-Hour Supermarkets: **Cala Foods** (California & Hyde, 776-3650; Stanyan & Haight, 752-3940; 1245 So. Van Ness & 23rd St., 282-0514). **Safeway** (15 Marina Blvd, 563-4946; Market & Church, 861-7660).

24-Hour Gas Stations: **Downtown-Shell** (5th St. at Folsom); **Union 76** (1st St. at Harrison). **Haight-Chevron** (Fell at Masonic). **Richmond-BP** (19th Ave. at Judah); **Shell** (Geary at 9th Ave.). **Sunset-Chevron** (19th Ave. at Irving).

If your car's been towed, dial 553-1235. The evil address of shitty most-hated **City Tow** is 850 Bryant, Room 145, open for torture 24 hours. Expect to pay a king's ransom to get your car back.

If your pet becomes deathly ill, or is hit by a car, take it to **Pets Unlimited Veterinary Hospital** (2343 Fillmore at Washington, 563-6700). They offer 24-hour emergency services, as well as a low-cost vaccination clinic for dogs and cats by appointment.

HEALTH & WELL-BEING

HIV/AIDS — For up-to-date, accurate information about prevention, testing, and early care and treatment of HIV/AIDS, call the **AIDS Hotline** (863-2437). To obtain information about getting tested anonymously, or to make an appointment, call the **AIDS Health Project**'s appointment line (502-8378). The San Francisco **AIDS Foundation** provides free direct and specialized services to persons living with AIDS and symptomatic HIV in San Francisco (487-3000).

Haight-Ashbury Free Medical Clinic — (558 Clayton at Haight, 487-5632) provides no-to-low cost basic medical services by appointment only.

American College of Traditional Chinese Medicine — (450 Connecticut, 282-9603) offers free and extremely low-cost acupuncture done by licensed acupuncturists. Of course, there'll be students observing, but hey, it's a great deal.

Iyengar Yoga Institute of San Francisco — (Taraval at 27th Ave., 753-0909) has free weekly yoga classes. Call for schedule.

Haight-Ashbury Free Detox Clinic — (529 Clayton at Haight, 565-1908) offers free detox programs for heroin, speed, cocaine, alcohol, and anything else that one can get addicted to.

Alcoholics Anonymous — (674-1821) Get info on where the meetings are happening.

General Hospital — (1001 Potrero at 23rd St., 206-8000) can be a true challenge, but if you don't have insurance, go there in an emergency whether it's physical or mental.

University of the Pacific Dental School (2155 Webster at Sacramento, 929-6501) — Free and low-cost services if your teeth are messed up, or even if they just haven't been cleaned in awhile.

SF Department of Human Services — (1235 Mission at 8th St., 557-5000). Bring a picture ID and social security card to get food stamps, and/or general assistance (also known as GA, or welfare).

Northern California Community Services Council (HELPLINK) — (772-4357) provides information on free food, shelter, and other services in case everything falls apart at once.

St. Martin de Porres House (225 Potrero at 16th St., 552-0240) serves free vegetarian breakfasts and lunches at their daily soup kitchen. Showers are also available twice a week.

In the miserable case where you need a lawyer, try the **Bay Area Legal Aid**, which provides free appeal help for tenant/landlord disputes, domestic violence, and public benefits (50 Sell at Van Ness, 982-1300 or 800-551-5554) or the Bar Association of **SF's Referral & Volunteer Legal Services Program** (989-1616).

Consumer Action (7171 Market, 777-9635) helps people

who've been screwed over. They can refer you to the appropriate complaint and licensing bureaus.

Consumer Credit Counseling Service (150 Post at Grant, 5th floor, 808-7526) helps people who have maxed out their credit cards and are up to their eyeballs in debt.

The **Main Post Office** (go out on 3rd past Army, and take a left on Evans, go half a block til you see the sign) is awesome. On weekdays, the counter's open til 8:30 p.m. and mail gets picked up until 11 p.m. weekdays and Saturdays, essential if you desperately need something postmarked by a certain date. If you're searching for a zip code, call 800-ASK-USPS. Call that same number to get directions to the post office at **SF International Airport** Post Office – it's open almost 24 hours a day and postmarks anything until 11 p.m.

If you want to adopt a pet, check with your landlord first, and then go to the **City Animal Shelter** (1200 15th St. at Harrison, 554-6364). They have a huge assortment of cats and dogs as well as guinea pigs, birds, and hamsters. The adoption fees are very reasonable, and these animals will be put to sleep if no one takes them home. The **SPCA** (2500 16th St. at Harrison, 554-3000) is right around the corner, if you don't see one you like at the City Shelter.

If you need to borrow a car for a few hours to move stuff or do a big shop at Rainbow Grocery or whatever, **City Carshare** (410 Jessie, 995-8588, www.citycarshare.org) has a program of car lending where anyone can borrow a car by the hour from various locations throughout the city. A $300 deposit is required and fees are by the hour and mile. No mileage charge if you borrow one of their electric cars.

DETOX & REHAB

If you or someone who know needs help kicking a drug habit , here are a few places that can help:

San Francisco 24-Hour Drug Abuse Crisis Line (Drug Line: 362-3400. Relapse Prevention: 834-1144)

Target Cities (1663 Mission, Second Floor. 24-hour information and crisis line: 800-750-2727. Monday-Friday, 8 a.m. - 5 p.m)

Haight Ashbury Free Medical Clinic Drug Detox Rehab and Aftercare Program (529 Clayton, 565-1908. Weekdays, 10 a.m. - 6 p.m. Free, drop-in programs.)

Westside Community Mental Health Center's Methadone Detox and Maintenance Center (1301 Pierce St., 563-8200. Open weekdays 7 a.m. - 3:30 p.m., weekends and holidays 8:30 -10:30 a.m.) Current legal ID required, over 18 only.

Bay Area Addiction Research and Treatment (BAART) (1040 Geary. 928-7800. Open weekdays 7-10:45 a.m., 12-2:15 p.m., except Wednesdays, open till 1 p.m. Weekends and holiday 8 a.m. - noon)

MAKING A FASHION STATEMENT

San Francisco has its own weather patterns — often the fog won't burn off till noon and will reappear with a vengeance around 3. Meteorological conditions can vary radically between neighborhoods — it may be 20 degrees colder in the Haight than the Mission. Dressing in layers is suggested. For additional warmth or accessories, the following shops specialize in eclectic selections of wearables.

New • Everyone loves a bargain and bargains abound throughout this town. Outlet and discount shopping is different than cruising into Nordstrom where there are racks of everything in ten sizes and five colors. If you can't resist Nordstrom, the **Nordstrom Rack** (Bryant at 9th St., 934-1211) is their local outlet. But with a little perseverance,

amazing finds can be discovered. Favorite outlets include:
Burlington Coat Factory (899 Howard at 5th St., 495-7234)
has lots more than coats, tons of clothes for everyone. **Shoe Pavilion** (974-1821) is in the same building.

There are many outlet stores south of Market in an area centered around Brannan & Bryant, and 2nd & 3rd Streets. Whether you're looking for a wedding dress or anything else, the area is certainly worth exploring.

Don't forget to check out **Marshall's** (901 Market at 5th St., 974-5368) and **Ross** (799 Market at 4th St., 957-9222), located one block apart, for some decent discounts off regular retail on clothes, shoes, and more. **Loehmann's** (222 Sutter at Kearny, 982-3215) also has great discount prices, whether you need a formal evening gown or a casual jacket.

Used • You'll be stylin' in the finest duds if you eschew the department stores and frequent the following shops. Choose between funky and extra-funky.

Next-to-New Shop (2226 Fillmore at Clay, 567-1627) is sponsored by the Junior League and has really good men's suits and fine clothing for women at very very reasonable prices. Need a suit for that wedding or business convention? This is the place to go! Couture stuff, too.

Clothes Contact (473 Valencia at 16th St., 621-3212) sells an ever-changing assortment of previously-owned clothing sold by the pound — sweaters, coats, shirts, etc. $8/lb.

Haight Street between Masonic and Stanyan has many recycled/vintage clothing stores — take a stroll, check 'em out — **Buffalo Exchange** (1555 Haight at Clayton, 431-

7733) will even buy choice clothes from you for cash or store credit.

Wacky thrift stores abound in the Mission — they're great for stocking a newly acquired living space with dishes, pots & pans, sheets, towels, etc. as well as clothes. Worth investigating are **Thrift Town** (2101 Mission at 17th St., 861-1132) and **Community Thrift** (623 Valencia at 17th St., 861-4910). **Salvation Army** (1509 Valencia at 26th St., 643-8040) and **Goodwill** (1580 Mission at So. Van Ness, 575-2240) stores are not too far away. The **Goodwill** at Bayview Plaza (Third St. and Evans) has great upscale designer label clothes cheap.

Furnishings • After a while having all of the furniture made out of milk crates and cinderblocks can get on your nerves. Besides the thrift stores, here are a few other good places to check out.

Express (1315 Howard at 9th St., 255-1311) They got the new couches with the funky patterns for a lot less than you'd pay elsewhere. Spent my first Christmas bonus there getting real furniture. Also try www.craigslist.com under Barter/Trade/Free listings. Lots of rich people give away their furniture for free if you can come get it.

Economy Restaurant Fixtures (1200 7th St. near Townsend, 626-5611) has good reasonably priced kitchen chairs, plates, cups, pots and pans, etc.

Cookin' (339 Divisadero at Oak, 861-1854) is one of the City's greatest stores for cooks - it features top-of-the-line used kitchen stuff (pots, pans, bakeware, you name it) at very reasonable prices. A tiny shop, things are crammed into every corner and it can be a real treasure hunt. Total fun, it's one of the places that makes San Francisco great!

Cottrell's (150 Valencia at Duboce, 431-1000) has been around forever and they have tons of quality used furniture at good prices.

For the coolest guitar shop in the Bay Area, **Subway Guitars** (1800 Cedar at Grant, Berkeley, 510-841-4106) wins hands down. In San Francisco, **Real Guitars** (15 Lafayette at Mission, 552-3310) also has used guitars and amplifiers and does repairs. **Guitar Center** (1321 Mission at 9th St., 626-7655) has good prices on new equipment, strings, etc.

For film, dark room supplies, and photo stuff, **Photographer's Supply** (436 Bryant at 2nd St., 979-0950) has the best prices in town.

If you enjoy the great outdoors, the **North Face Outlet** (1325 Howard at 9th St., 626-6444) has a great selection of camping and hiking gear. For running, tennis, and basketball sneakers, there's **Big 5 Sporting Goods** (1533 Sloat at 34th Ave., 681-4593).

Scroungers' Center for Reusable Art Parts (SCRAP) (Newcomb Alley off Toland, 647-1746, Tues.-Thurs. 9-5) has all kinds of paper, cloth, metal, wood, and glass bits and pieces that changes daily based on what's been donated. They also have just weird junk, some of it free, everything else super low-cost that's good for arts and crafts, and other creative projects.

For sex toys and erotic goodies, go to **Good Vibrations Store** (1210 Valencia at 23rd St., 974-8980), which is geared toward women and men. Owned and operated by women, **Stormy Leather** (1158 Howard at 8th St., 626-1672) specializes in bondage and fetish gear.

CHEAP EATS
BY
STEPHANIE ROSENBAUM

THE MISSION - First of all there are burritos. If there were no burritos, no indie filmmakers/spoken-word poets/bike messengers/bodyworker-herbal healers would be able to live here. For size, cheapness, and sheer calories per square inch, San Francisco's burritos are every cheap eater's best friend. You can find taquerias all over the city, but most of the best ones are still in the Mission. **El Toro** (598 Valencia at 17th St., 431-3351), **Pancho Villa** (307 116th St., at Valencia, 864-8840), and **Taqueria Can-Cun** (2288 Mission at 19th, 252-9560) routinely sweep all the free newsweeklies' best-burrito contests, and you'd have to pile on a lot of extra sour cream and guacamole to spend more than $5 per meal. **La Taqueria** (2889 Mission at 25th St., 285-7117) does just three things: quesadillas, tacos, and burritos, but all are awesomely good. Just don't expect rice - it's a strictly a meat-beans-salsa operation, which, for meat lovers, is a good thing: more carne for your buck. At **Casa Sanchez** (2778 24th St. at York, 282-2400), you can sit outside on the back patio and pig out on homemade tortilla chips dunked in the best salsa in the city. Off the burrito beat, **Chava's** (3248 18th St., at Shotwell, 552-9387) offers big platters of huevos rancheros or huevos Mexicanas in the morning. The caldo de pollo, brimming with a least a full bird's worth of chicken in a steamy, spicy broth, can cure whatever ails you. On weekends, order the menudo (tripe soup) - reputed to be a surefire hangover cure or the birria (stewed goat), which tastes like really butch brisket. The perennially cool hangout **El Rio** (3158 Mission at Cesar Chavez, 282-3325) offers free all-you-can-eat oysters from 5-7 p.m. on Fridays, plus lots of good hot shake-what-your-mamma-gave-you worldbeat music. After you've had a few pints, scarfed oysters, and danced, head next door to **El Zocalo** (3230 Mission at Valencia, 282-2572), which stays open really late serving good, inexpensive Salvadorean food. Order lots of the hot, melty cheese- or pork-stuffed pupusas, which are super-cheap and come with a tangy shredded cabbage salad, which will help con you into thinking you're eating something healthy. Also right nearby is **Brisas de Acapulco** (3137 Mission at Cesar Chavez, 826-1496) which offers huge portions of fresh seafood, like eyeballs-and-all whole fried fish, brimming bowls of chunky fish soups and ceviche-style chilled seafood cocktails. The tiny Caribbean-flavored **El Nuevo Frutilandia** (3077 24th St. at Folsom, 648-2958) has a great deal on Cuban sandwiches at lunchtime (and very tasty Cuban/Puerto Rican food at dinnertime), while **Mom Is Cooking** (1166 Geneva at Edinburgh, 586-7000), over in the Excelsior district, is known for its super-fluffy tamales, which you can enjoy with a margarita or two outside in the back garden they've dubbed "Mom's Patio".

For take-out tamales, try the Mexican, Salvadorean, or Nicaraguan versions available at **La Palma Mexicatessen** (2884 24th St. at Florida, 647-1500). Cute, funky **Cafe Abo** (3369 Mission at 30th) has great coffee and a very creative organic sandwich menu, while **Zante Indian Pizzeria** (3489 Mission at Cortland, 821-3949) gives fusion food a good, garlicky name. Their Indian pizza—covered with spicy spinach, cauliflower, and tandoori chicken (there's a vegetarian version too)—is a great way to surmount those don't-know-what-to-have dilemmas. It's Indian food! It's pizza! Everybody's happy. For hipster dates, try **Emmy's Spaghetti Shack** (18 Virginia at Mission, 206-2086), perhaps the only place in town with a DJ, $5 spag and meatballs, and both merlot and Mickey's on the bar menu. Over in the Northeast Mission, (surrounded by what used to be looming industrial warehouses, now big lofts and big offices for whatever dot-coms are hanging on their last shreds of VC cash) is **Hung Yen** (3100 18th St. at Harrison, 621-8531), where you can enjoy cheap, tasty Vietnamese eats out on the plant-shaded patio. Back on Mission Street, you can smell **Pete's BBQ** (2399 Mission at 20th, 826-1009) from halfway down the block. The Greek guys who run the place know that every chicken's better for a little lemon and oregano, and every chicken's best when it's cooked in a rotisserie in the window, so hungry customers can see (and smell) their dinner before they even know they want it. A big piece of moist, juicy bird, salad, bread, and a baked potato the size of your foot, all for less than six bucks.

Eating cheap over on Valencia is another story. It was a true low point for the Mission when the scruffy, surly, but huge-portioned New Dawn Cafe closed and a trendy sushi joint opened in its place. What used to get you a bottomless cup of coffee and a huge platter of veggie scramble with home fries and a biscuit as big as your pillow now buys two little pieces of raw fish. New places opening in this formerly affordable neighborhood will charge you $8 just to valet-park your car. Luckily, the guys at the hallway-sized **Truly Mediterranean** (1309 16th St. at Valencia, 252-7482) still sing as they roll up your huge and delicious falafel, hummus, or shawerma sandwich. Along with their original tiny location next to the Roxie Cinema, they've got a place in North Beach (627 Vallejo at Columbus, 362-2636), and both spots can't be beat for cheap Middle Eastern eats, especially the lamb-kebab wrap. The French ciders, onion soup, and thin, toasty buckwheat crepes at **Ti Couz** (3108 16th St. at Valencia, 252-7373) are the real item, and the seafood salad is deceptively bountiful (just be sure to come here at off hours to beat the constant lines) For Indian, the menu (and ambiance) at **Pakwan** (3180 16th St. at Valencia, 776-0160) is bare-bones (order at the counter, wait for your number to be called) but the naan bread is fresh and hot, the tandoori lamb chops are great, and the prices show that they're not wasting your cash on anything silly like decor. For something snackier, follow the waft of cumin in the air to **Bombay Bazaar** (548 Valencia at 16th, 621-1717), an Indian grocery/general store. If you want a Ganeesh incense burner, stick-on sparkly bindis, or ghee in a jar, you'll find it here; if you want a cheap, yummy snack, go next door to the brightly painted take-out shop, **Bombay Ice Creamery** (552 Valencia at 16th, 431-1103), where they offer a short menu of Indian chaats - small, soupy combinations of samosas, chickpeas, yogurt, and various vegetables or chicken. And for much less than the price of a pint of Chunky Monkey, you can walk out with a cup of Indian ice cream, which come in brilliant sari colors to match flavors like rose petal, mango, lychee, fig, and cardamom. **Arinell Pizza** (509 Valencia at 16th, 255-1303) is as close as you'll get to a New York-style slices joint. Very thin, foldable crust, normal toppings like mushrooms or pepperoni, and no atmosphere beyond a list of prices and a few stools. And **Big Mouth Burgers** (3392 24th St. at Valencia, 821-4821) has a chipper, friendly staff and a tasty burger on a toasted bun that comes with great fries, baked beans, or slaw for around $5. They also do a great veggie burger, as well as a good, goopy grilled vegetable sandwich on foccacia. For dates, try the sexy **Luna Park** (694 Valencia at 18th St., 553-8584) opened by a couple of Chow alumni. Great mojitos, sprightly little salads, solid California-bistro entrees, and do-it-yourself s'mores for dessert. If you want to swap sweet nothings, ask for the alcove table in the back—sit anywhere else and you'll be shouting across the table.

THE TENDERLOIN - Gentrification hasn't washed the junkies and SRO hotels out of the Tenderloin yet, which means the neighb', while definitely dicey in parts, is still a source of great cross-cultural cheap eats. Colonialism has many evils to answer for; then again, the French influence in Vietnam did produce the banh mi, or Vietnamese sandwich, to the delight of starving students everywhere. A fat, crusty French roll is warmed to toastiness, then slapped with mayo and stuffed with exuberant amounts of barbecued pork, pork pate, grilled 5-spice chicken, or "fancy pork" (a pale, spongy cold cut), sprigs of fresh cilantro, and crunchy vinegared shards of carrots, onions, and daikon radish. **Saigon Sandwiches** (560 Larkin at Eddy, 474-5698) makes particularly good ones for about $2 each, as does the larger and more decked-out **Wrap Delight Vietnam Sandwiches** (426 Larkin at Golden Gate, 771-3388) opened recently by a couple of former Saigon Sandwiches employees.

If you'd like a more sit-down kind of meal, head to **Them Key** (717 Ellis at Larkin, 441-8525) for pho (pronounced sort of like "fwa"), a bucket-sized bowl of beef broth loaded with curly rice noodles and all kinds of meat (anything from flank steak to tendon and tripe.) Garnished to taste with sprigs of fresh cilantro, purple Thai basil, mint, and wedges of lime, pho will make your tastebuds do a little dance, right there under the fluorescent lights. Along the counter you'll see a pastel rainbow of plastic cups filled with every color and flavor of bubble tea—iced tea mixed with sweetened condensed milk and chubby black "pearls" of slippery tapioca, slurped through an extra-wide straw. **Golden Flower** (667 Jackson at Kearny, 433-6469), another pint-sized but always bustling Vietnamese place, also dishes out a really excellent pho, along with cold rice-paper wrapped salad rolls and high-octane Vietnamese iced coffee. For Thai food, squeeze into the extremely petite **BKK Thai** (1022 Bush at Leavenworth, 441-8150) or into the bigger, bustling **Osha Thai Noodle Cafe** (696 Geary at Leavenworth, 673-2368), which is clean, speedy, and more hipster-populated than the rest of the neighborhood's Formica-and-fluorescence joints (it's also open til 1 a.m. weekdays, 3 a.m. on weekends).

    Shalimar (523 Jones at Geary, 928-0333), also in the 'Loin, serves great Indian food for very little cash. Unlike like a lot of cheap Indian places, Shalimar makes everything to order, which means no goopy steam-table murk, and their smoking-hot flatbreads make great scoops. The Pakistani bent of the place means meats are a specialty, especially the chicken, lamb, and ground-lamb seekh kebabs done in the tandoor oven. **Naan 'N Curry** nearby (478 O'Farrell at Jones, 775-1349) has slightly less chaos and cooking smoke, and lots of rich, stewy dishes full of butter-tender lamb and long-cooked things like okra that are delicious, oily proof that sometimes a relaxed vegetable is a tastier vegetable. No one goes home hungry from the long counter at **Soups** (784 O'Farrell at Larkin, 775-6406), where benevolent owner Richard makes his homemade soups from scratch every day, and every bowl comes with lots of crackers and a free refill.

DOWNTOWN - Everyone, even Julia Child (look for the yellowed newspaper write-up on the wall), loves **Tu Lan** (8 6th St. at Market, 626-0927) a hole-in-the-wall Vietnamese joint on skanky Sixth Street. The soups, cold spring rolls, hot deep-fried imperial rolls, and crunchy stir-fried noodles are still good; too often, other dishes are just sweet and greasy. Then again, Tu Lan's cheap and a real local fave (unlike the totally touristic **House of Nanking** (919 Kearny at Columbus, 421-1429), which is really, really not worth the huge wait it takes to get into this completely overhyped dive). [Editor's note: Hey, I like House of Nanking... if you go during odd hours - lunch at 2 p.m. - there's no line, and the Nanking Shrimp does for sweet potatoes what Jimi Hendrix did for the guitar.] For a taste of what the waterfront was like before Pac Bell Park and the microbrew places muscled their way into Mission Bay and South Beach, duck into **Red's Java House** (Pier 28 on the Embarcadero, no phone). Regular working-Joe food, like long-neck Buds and double cheeseburgers, real cheap. Outside, awesome-industrial views of the Bay Bridge. If you're (lucky enough to still be) working for the Man down in the Financial District, the cheapest sandwiches (made with good stuff—real turkey, nice tuna salad, decent salami) can be found at **Lee's Deli**, which has numerous branches (look for the red-and-white awnings) all around downtown. For cheap takeout sushi, soba and udon noodle soups, and chicken teriyaki, line up at **Yo Yo's** (318 Pacific at Battery, 296-8273), then go stretch out in the sun in nearby Walton Park (at Pacific and Front Streets).

SOUTH OF MARKET - Philly-style cheesesteaks star at **WhizWit** (1525 Folsom at 11th St., 558-9200). The food at **Brainwash** (1122 Folsom at 7th St., 437-2363) isn't cheap (although they do a surprisingly good veggie burger) but you can do your wash at the same time, so if time is money, the extra couple bucks you'll spend to get a grilled-chicken salad might be worth it. For a date, **Le Charm** (315 5th St. at Folsom, 546-6128) is true to its name, offering satisfying, very affordable French food and loads of low-key Gallic charm. (Drive or take a cab here so the bleak, windswept concrete avenues outside don't harsh your candlelit buzz).

THE AVENUES - In the Inner Sunset, you can get a big whomping salad or a busting-out sandwich on thick-cut, homemade whole wheat bread at **Einstein's Cafe** (1336 9th Ave. at Irving, 665-4840), a cheerful (check out the physics graffiti on the lime green walls) little spot that also gives on-the-job training to local teens. For those rare non-foggy Sunset afternoons, take your tray out to the peaceful duplex patio out back. For all-around eats, you can't go wrong at nearby **Park Chow** (1240 9th Ave. at Irving, 665-9912) or its Church Street sister **Chow** (215 Church at Market, 552-2469) except that it's pretty much always packed. When you finally get a table, though, there are swell thin-crust pizzas (made in the wood-burning oven), generous pastas that veer from Asian-inspired "smiling noodles" to Ragu-ad spaghetti and meatballs, and great homemade butterscotch-banana pie. Plus, they've got beer on tap and nifty fresh juices. About 10 blocks west, you can warm up with a huge bowl o'beef, broth and noodles at **Pho Hoa-Hiep II** (1833 Irving at 19th Ave., 664-0469) for around the price of a grande mocha Frappucino. Up along Clement Street in the Richmond, you'll find dozens of hole-in-the-wall Asian restaurants and dim sum shops. Shrimp dumplings are three for a dollar at **Good Luck Dim Sum** (738 Clement St. at 8th Ave., 386-3388) — perfect for fueling an afternoon lost in the stacks at nearby Green Apple Books, the Winchester Mystery House of used bookstores. **Wing Lee** (503 Clement St. at 6th Ave., 668-9481) also has tasty, cheap take-out dim sum as well as good-quality prepared food, like glossy-skinned roast ducks. For almost-as-cheap sit-down eats, check out **Burma Super Star** (309 Clement at 4th Ave., 387-2147) or order a bowl of noodles with roasted duck at **King of Thai Noodle House** (639 Clement at 6th Ave., 752-5198). **Thai Time** (315 8th Ave. at Clement, 831-3663) is tiny and cute, with very good curries, soups, and specials, like pumpkin-seafood curry, that are worth breaking out of your pad Thai/tom ka gai rut for. **Old Mandarin Islamic restaurant** (3132 Vincente at 42nd Ave., 564-3481) is way out in the very Outer Sunset but offers ribsticking, cold-weather Mandarin cuisine (lamb hot pot, a communal, cooked-at-the-table affair, is only on the Chinese-language menu, but it's worth requesting when you've got a hungry group; also try the beef tongue and Peking beef pie) that's very different from the usual Cantonese fare seen around the city. **Java Restaurant** (417 Clement at 5th Avenue, 752-1541) restaurant in the Richmond has Indonesian noodles with peanut sauce and satays really cheap, and their spicy french fries are sheer delight. For a taste of grandmother Russia, duck into the **Cinderella Bakery** (436 Balboa at 5th Ave., 751-9690) for borscht and piroshki.

Heading out to the beach? Get your grub at the whimsical **Sea Biscuit Cafe** (3815 Noriega at 45th Ave., 661-3784) or stop in for coffee at Java Beach (1396 La Playa at Judah, 665-5282), a surfers' hangout located right next to the N-Judah turnaround. Both have sandwiches, soups, and the occasional bowl o'chili or plate of lasagna to go with the usual coffees, cookies, and bagels.

NORTH BEACH AND CHINATOWN - Speaking of noodles, most of the spaghetti joints in North Beach are overpriced and generic. Instead of spending 10 or 12 bucks on what you could make at home with a box of Ronzoni and a jar of Classico, go for the thin-crust pizzas, roast pork, or foccacia sandwiches at **L'Osteria del Forno** (519 Columbus at Union, 982-1124), the old-style pizzas (baked in a wood-burning brick oven) at **Tommaso's** (1042 Kearny at Broadway, 398-9696), or the deep-dish, fat slices displayed in the window of the very punk rock **Golden Boy Pizzeria** (542 Green at Stockton, 982-9738). In case you're wondering, the green ones are clam and garlic - potent, but good. Among all the noodle joints are old-fashioned restaurants still serving "Italian dinners", which means everyone gets antipasti, bread, soup and salad ladled out of big no-nonsense metal bowls, followed by pasta—and then they'll ask you what you want for dinner. The answer's solid Italian-American fare like eggplant Parmesan and chicken cacciatore, served up to hearty eaters at **Capp's Corner** (1600 Powell at Green, 989-2589) or **Gold Spike Restaurant** (527 Columbus at Union, 421-4591), both of which have been around forever and still won't charge you much over $12 for a complete dinner. **Mo's Burgers** (1322 Grant Ave at Vallejo, 415-788-3779) is the place to go when all the other restaurants have lines and you need to eat now. The vegetarian Grant Avenue sandwich, a combination of garlicky grilled mushrooms and fresh avocado served on foccacia, is served with a mound of excellent fries for under $7. And if you want a little titillation with your eats, the Lusty Lady is one of the 'hood's last old-fashioned quarter-in-the-slot peep shows. They're also the only nudie place on the strip with unionized dancers. With the bucks you're saving, you can chow down til nearly 3 a.m. at **Yuet Lee** (1300 Stockton at Broadway, 982-6020), a lime-green, fluorescent-lit Chinese place on the cusp of Chinatown. Good salt and pepper squid, fresh seafood, and ginger noodles. Or you can try out **Silver Restaurant** (737 Washington at Grant, 434-4998), which serves dim sum until midnight. **Hon's Wun Tun House** (648 Kearny at Clay, 433-3966) has wonderfully flavorful soup broths with won ton noodles as well as good no-frills Chinese food for less than $5 a plate. Try **New Hong Kong Menu** (667 Commercial at Kearny, 391-3677) for noodles, or **Young's Cafe** (601 Kearny at Sacramento, 397-3455) for Cantonese dishes for around $4 to $5 a plate. **Golden Star** (11 Walter Lum Place at Grant, Kearny and Clay, 398-1215) will sate your Vietnamese pho cravings for around $4 a bowl. **Molinari Delicatessen** (373 Columbus at Vallejo, 421-2337) is the godfather of all Italian delis; take a number, grab a roll from the bin, and order one of their huge specialty sandwiches. You'll end up with olive oil dripping all over your lap (and sleeves), but that's why you bought those pants at Ross to begin with, right?

WESTERN ADDITION AND PACIFIC HEIGHTS - You're bound to end up checking out the flicks at one of the many film festivals that end up at the Kabuki movie theater, so it's good to know where to get a cheap bite nearby. Head to Japantown, but skip the sushi in favor of - yep, you guessed it - noodles at **Mifune** (1737 Post at Geary, 922-0337), **Iroha** (1728 Buchanan at Post, 922-0321), or **Sapporo-Ya** (1531 Webster at Post, 563-7400). **Pride of the Mediterranean** (1761 Fillmore at Sutter, 567-1150) is a nice place (with belly dancers!) for sit-down Middle Eastern fare. For dates, check out one of the happy foreign flicks at the **Clay Theater** up on Fillmore Street, then try the homey **La Mediterranee**

(2210 Fillmore at Sacramento, 921-2956) for hummus, retisina and things wrapped in phyllo, or the chic **Chez Nous** (1911 Fillmore at Bush, 441-8044) which offers shareable plates of Spanish, Greek, and Provencal dishes and lots of delicious, crusty bread from its sister bakery, the Bay Bread Boulangerie down the street.

SUSHI - But what if you're craving that raw-fish protein high? For sushi that won't cost the rent (or taste like those shiny plastic maki in the window), it's easy to find a branch of the reliable, no-frills **We Be Sushi** (538 Valencia at 16th St., 565-0749; 1071 Valencia at 22nd St., 826-6607; 3226 Geary, Parker, 221-9960; 94 Judah at 6th Ave., 681-4010). Or try **Nippon** (a.k.a. No-Name) **Sushi** (314 Church at 15th St., no phone), or wacky **Country Station Sushi** (2140 Mission, at Sycamore, 861-0972). Eschewing the trapping of trendy sushi joints, the tiny **Yum Yum Fish** (2181 Irving at 23nd Ave., 566-6433) offers fresh, reliable raw seafood as well as very affordable sushi (mostly to go). Don't be fooled by the big, tacky plastic "Sushi Sake" sign outside **Minako** (2154 Mission at 17th, 864-1888). Inside, this tiny mother-daughter venture offers a fresh, well-prepared sushi selection, as well as lots of really good Japanese home cooking with vegetarian/vegan options way beyond the usual seaweed salads and cucumber rolls.

BREAKFAST - For breakfast, the rule of thumb is this: a place named after a guy will get you busted vinyl booths, little plastic thimbles of creamer with the coffee, and your basic toast, eggs, and meat for cheap e.g., **Jim's Restaurant** (2420 Mission at 20th St., 285-6020), **Eddie's Cafe** (800 Divisadero, 563-9780), **Hungry Joe's** (1748 Church at 29th St. , 282-7333), **Al's Good Food Cafe** (3286 Mission at 29th, 641-8445), where the salsa rules, and the open-round-the-clock **Orphan Andy's** (3991 17th St. at Castro, 864-9795). A woman's name will get you fancier pancakes, more fruit, more fresh vegetables, and a higher tab. If it's too pretty a day for a greasy spoon, cruise into **Chloe's Cafe** (1399 Church at 26th St., 648-4116), **Dottie's True Blue Cafe** (522 Jones at Geary, 885-2767), which is kitschy and cute, even if its proximity to Union Square's hotels means lots of glittery sweatshirts and Alcatraz baseball caps on the clientele. Potrero Hill's hallway-sized **Just for You** (1483 18th St. at Connecticut, 647-3033) makes its own cornbread and thick-cut English-muffin bread; they also make great breakfast burritos, and you can get spicy crab cakes or grits with your eggs. Wherever you get your morning chow, if you don't want to spend your weekend hours cooling your Docs out on the sidewalk with the rest of the surly, uncaffeinated hordes, do your best to roll out of bed before 11 a.m. **Boogaloo's** (3296 22nd St. at Valencia, 824-3211), **All You Knead** (1466 Haight at Masonic, 552-4550), and the **Pork Store Cafe** (1451 Haight at Ashbury, 864-6981) all offer a multi-pierced staff, massive omelettes, and huge coma-inducing bowls of home fries doused with sour cream, cheese, and salsa. The **Ebb Tide Cafe** (1500 South Van Ness at 26th, 643-4399) has really good food (with nice touches like real maple syrup and homemade sausages) at close-to-Formica-counter prices. Don't be suckered by the super-authentic looking It's Tops diner; it's known by locals as either It's OK or, more frankly, It Sucks. It's too bad the food is so greasy and service are so lame, because they do have those cool boothside jukeboxes.

DIM SUM ETC. - If you're in the mood for something a little less predictable than the usual tower o'spuds, Chinatown and Clement Street (in the Richmond) are rife with cheapo daytime dim sum joints. Big fluffy white bbq pork buns, translucent shrimp dumplings, porky sui mai, silky scallion-studded rice crepes - you can get them for about a dollar an order at **Good Luck Dim Sum** (736 Clement at 8th Ave., 386-3388) or grungy but good **Dol Ho** (808 Pacific at Stockton, 392-2828). The deli-counter style places, like Good Luck, are cheaper; places where you choose off rolling carts may be a little more expensive, but they'll usually have fresher and more varied offerings. **Gold Mountain** (644 Broadway at Grant, 296-7733) is huge and usually crowded, but service is speedy and the dim sum amazingly good. Two can satisfy their every pork-bun or chicken-feet craving and still get change back from a twenty. For the ultimate Chinese comfort food, sink your spoon into the congee (savory rice porridge) served with fried crullers at **Hing Ling** (674 Broadway at Stockton, 398-8838) or go vegetarian at the shoebox-sized **Lucky Creation** (854 Washington at Grant, 989-0818) where even hardcore veggies can be guilt-free carnivores for the night, thanks to the many faux-meat dishes. Mmm, gluten duck skin!

BOOZE BALLAST - For cheap eats with your booze, margaritas come by the pitcherful at **Puerto Alegre** (546 Valencia at 16th, 255-8201) and **La Rondalla** (901 Valencia at 20th, 647-7474). But stick to the guac and chips at La Rondalla - even though it's always Christmas in the heavily kitschified dining room, the lard-heavy food can be pretty nasty.

Edinburgh Castle (950 Geary at Larkin, 885-4074), a Scottish pub with cool live shows, gets an extra dose of authenticity by having a delivery arrangement with the nearby Chelsea Fish and Chips; put in an order at the bar and a few minutes later a hot newspaper-wrapped bundle will come right to your table, ready for salt and a shot of malt vinegar.

Got a buddy in a band? See if they can get a Sunday-afternoon gig at **Bottom of the Hill** (4-8pm, Sundays, 1233 17th St. at Missouri, 621-4455), where six bucks gets you a paper plate full of all-you-can-eat barbecue to go with the live tunes. **El Rio** (3158 Mission at Cesar Chavez, 282-3325) offers free all-you-can-eat oysters from 5-7pm on Friday nights, plus a spacious outdoor patio (complete with a huge lemon tree and a Carmen Miranda mural) for al fresco shucking and slurping. **Zeitgeist** (199 Valencia at Duboce, 255-7505), a staunchly ungentrified biker (bicycles as well as motorcycles) bar has a funky beer garden out back where the owners often fire up the grill on sunny weekend afternoons (And for your visiting sleep-through-anything pals, they also have a few rooms upstairs that rent for $30 a night). In the summertime, weekends will often find the staff firing up a grill outside **Treat Street Cocktails** (3050 24th St. at Treat, 824-5954).

If you're drinking in the lower Haight, stumble out of Noc Noc or Toronado and pick up a sausage sandwich at **Rosamunde Grill** (545 Haight at Fillmore, 437-6851). German-style wursts are the specialty here, but all kinds of lamb, beef, duck, chicken, and seafood sausages are on display behind the glass counter, ready to be grilled and slapped into a dense, chewy bun and loaded up with sauerkraut, grilled onions, and mustard. Even better, pick up a sausage before you start drinking, and bring it into the bar to enjoy with a brew. Definitely plan to drop in here on Tuesday, when they also serve up amazing $4 cheeseburgers.

DONUTS - And finally, doughnuts. San Francisco is a city of many charms, but universally, the doughnuts suck. The only really good doughnuts are across the Golden Gate Bridge in Larkspur at a tiny place called **Donut Alley** (471 Magnolia, Larkspur, 924-4339). If you're heading north to check out Point Reyes, Mount Tam, Stinson Beach, or anything else in Marin County, it's completely worth a short detour off 101. Get on the road early, however, since they close when they sell out of doughnuts, around 11 a.m.

GROCERIES - Of course, the cheapest way to eat is to cook for yourself. Safeway and Cala Foods are convenient and great for stocking up on Cap't Crunch and cat food at 3 a.m., but you'll spend way too much money doing all your shopping at supermarkets. For stuff like lettuce and tomatoes and bananas (not to mention papayas and yams), head to Clement Street in the Richmond, Mission and 24th Streets in the Mission, or Stockton Street in Chinatown. All of these streets and their environs are dotted with fruit and vegetable stands offering good quality produce at way-below-supermarket prices. **New May Wah** (547 Clement at 6th Ave., 668-2583), has very fresh, very cheap Asian groceries and produce as well as meat, poultry, and fish (although you may have to elbow your way in past many determined grandmothers.) But what about rice, beans, and echinacea tincture? From the organic quinoa to the fifteen different kinds of seaweed, **Rainbow Grocery** (1745 Folsom at 13th St., 863-0620) is bulk-bin nirvana. Besides row after row of lentils, sea salt, granola, and falafel mix, you can also find cookbooks, cookware, rosemary-mint hair conditioner, organic-cotton sanitary pads, tons of excellent cheese and fancy olives, great (mostly organic, although not cheap) produce, and enough St. John's wort to turn Dostyevsky into Tony Robbins. If you cook a lot, you can save yourself serious bank by buying your spices here in bulk. A little jar of oregano or cinnamon can cost you three or four bucks at Safeway; here, the same stuff weighed out in a little paper bag goes for mere pennies. You can also find everything from a used motorcycle ("runs great!") to a room in a sunny nonsmoking dyke-friendly 2-cat household up for grabs on the bulletin-board wall. Other good things: Bike racks, a parking lot, and diaper-changing tables in both bathrooms. If you're having a party where (you hope) people will be trading witty banter instead of just heading straight for the keg, Trader Joe's (555 9th St., at Bryant, 863-1292; also 3 Masonic at Geary, 346-9964) is your one-stop party shop. Lots of little frozen hors d'oeuvre-y things like potstickers and mini-quiches, plus cheese, crackers, precut veggies, dip, vacuum-packed smoked salmon, cookies, and tons of good (and cheap) wine, beer, and liquor. Be careful not to get sucked in the cross-pollination of shopping opportunities at 9th and Brannan (Bed Bath and Beyond, Pier One, Nordstrom Rack) unless you want a serious big-box hangover by the end of the afternoon.

COFFEE - Someone in your household is bound to be working at Peets or 'Bucks, which means your freezer's probably already stocked with 20 lbs of Sumatra French Roast. But if not, **Castro Cheesery** (427 Castro at Market, 552-6676) has the best prices on coffee beans in the city, plus millions of teas, lots of cheese (natch) and many, many boxes of fancy European cookies, crackers, and chocolates.

FARMERS MARKETS - **Heart of the City Farmers Market**, (Civic Center Plaza, Market at 9th St., 558-9455). Wednesday and Sunday, 10 a.m. to 4 p.m. Very cheap, pretty scruffy, with a pungent reek from the fresh-fish trucks. Pick and choose what you put in your bag here, as the low prices mean the quality can be spotty. **Alemany Farmers Market** (100 Alemany at Bayshore, 647- 9423). Saturday 9 a.m. - 3 p.m. A very democratic market. Lots of Asian produce, more organics than Civic Center, but mostly just lots of good in-season produce at very reasonable (and sometimes super-cheap) prices. Do some comparison shopping through the stalls before you buy. Some favorites: very fresh eggs, long purple-green stalks of sugarcane, bread samples and raisin-cheese danishes from the Pan-O-Rama bakery. **Ferry Plaza Farmers Market** (Embarcadero at Green, 353-5650). Saturday, 8 a.m. - 1 p.m. The Neiman-Marcus of farmers markets. Lots of organically glamorous produce here. Everything here has a pedigree - that's not just a peach, it's an O'Henry peach from Frog Hollow Farms and probably one of the best peaches you've ever tasted, as it should be for three or four bucks a pound. Black radishes, purple potatoes, lettuce leaves that look like they've just been sprung from the preemie ward - you can tell which producers have Chez Panisse-anointed star status by the crowds around their booths. If you can't wait to get home to eat, there are short-order stands serving up scrambled eggs with smoked salmon or brioche French toast, as well as nontraditional morning fare like roasted mussels and salmon BLTs. Who goes: foodies, local chefs, lots of yuppie parents giving Caitlin and Zachary their very first taste of goat brie. Even if you don't feel like spending $5 a pound on organic wild-gathered baby arugula, you can taste your way through the best Northern California has to offer, as nearly every stand has free samples there for the munching. Even better, the always spotless F-Market vintage streetcars now run all the way from Market and Castro to Fisherman's Wharf, making a stop right next the market.

Of course, the best and cheapest way to get food is to grow it yourself. If you have a backyard, you'll quickly learn the delights of our year-round growing season (broccoli, kale, and chard will happily produce all winter; if you've got a warm enough place, you can have cherry tomatoes through October). No yard? Call up SLUG, the **San Francisco League of Urban Gardeners** (2080 Oakdale at Selby, 285-7584), and see if there's a plot open in a community garden near you. For a nominal fee, you can get your very own patch of ground, and for the price of an envelope of seeds, you can harvest fresh lettuce all winter. Keep an eye on your friends' backyards, too. Do they have a tree with lemons or plums free for the picking? Ripening in late August or September, blackberries grow wild all over the city, especially in the northern, sandy areas near the water. Just be careful of poison oak, which often grows hand-in-hand with blackberries.

EDITOR'S PICKS

Korean BBQ - For the best in interactive eating, check out a Korean BBQ joint. Not cheap but total fun with pals, as the table is immediately covered in little dishes featuring bean sprouts, kim chee, tiny dried fish, and several less identifiable items. After deciding which kind of marinated meat you'd prefer (this type of restaurant is not recommended for vegetarians), a guy comes running out of the kitchen carrying a hibachi filled with blazing hot charcoal. He sets it on your table and the fun begins. Most of these places are on Geary Blvd out in the avenues, including **Kyoung Bok Palace** (6314 Geary at 27th Ave).

Vegetarian - Veggies can have an awesome time eating out in this town: in Chinatown, there's **Lucky Creation Vegetarian Restaurant** (854 Washington at Grant, 989-0818). Then there's the **Shangri-La Chinese Vegetarian Restaurant** (2026 Irving at 21st Ave., 731-2548) in the Outer Sunset, and **Bamboo Garden Vegetarian Restaurant** (832 Clement at 6th Ave., 876-0832) in the Inner Richmond. **The Ganges** (775 Frederick at Arguello, 661-7290) features delicious all-vegetarian Indian cuisine.

All-You-Can-Eats - AYCE pizza and salad at **Goat Hill**

Pizza (300 Connecticut at 18th, 641-1440) on Monday nights for $8.50. **Umeko** Japanese Seafood Buffet Restaurant (Japantown, 22 Peace Plaza, 776-1491; 1675 Post at Laguna) has a AYCE Asian seafood buffet every night for $17.95, including sushi. **Original Buffalo Wings** (663 Union at Columbus, 296-9907) has AYCE guess what (buffalo wings, duh) for $7.99 on Wednesdays, 4-9 p.m.

Open 24 Hours – At some point, you're gonna need to eat at 4 a.m. and you'll wonder what's open. In Chinatown, there's the **Silver Restaurant** (737 Washington at Grant, 433-8888). Clubhoppers' joints include the **Bagdad Cafe** (2295 Market at 16th St., 621-4434), **Orphan Andy's** (3991 17th at Market, 864-9795), and **Sparky's** (242 Church at Market, 626-8666). Otherwise, the following places are open 'round the clock. None of 'em are great, but at 5 a.m. who cares? **Silver Crest Donut Shop** (340 Bayshore at Oakdale, 826-0753); **Lucky Penny** (2670 Geary at Masonic, 921-0836); **Video Cafe** (5700 Geary at 21st, 387-3999); **Denny's Japantown** (1700 Post at Laguna, 563-1400); **International House of Pancakes** (2299 Lombard at Pierce, 921-4004); **Mel's Diner** (2165 Lombard, 921-3039) is open 24 hours on Fridays and Saturdays. **North Beach Pizza** (1499 Grant Ave at Union, 433-2444) delivers until two a.m.

Ice Cream - Great frozen confections abound throughout town: **Mitchell's** (688 San Jose at 29th, 648-2300); **Double Rainbow** (519 Powell at Sutter, 982-3097; 68 West Portal at Vincent, 564-9412); **Ben & Jerry's** (1480 Haight at Ashbury, 626-4143; and 543 Columbus at Union, 249-4684); **Bombay Ice Creamery** (552 Valencia, 431-1103), but **Rite Aid** drugstores (776 Market, 397-0837; and 1830 Ocean Av., 333-5135) still offer huge cones for 99 cents.

WATERING HOLES

GOING UP • Achieving Momentum through Proper Caffeination • There are way too many awesome cafes where local poets have found inspiration at the bottom of a latte glass, so here are a few of the venerable coffeehouses with personality that transcend trendy twiddle-twaddle:

North Beach's oldest, crustiest **Caffe Trieste** (601 Vallejo at Grant, 392-6739) is visited daily by poets, filmmakers, and other bohemian and wannabes. Get a cap to go and sit on the church steps across the street for unique neighborhood observations.

Sacred Grounds (2095 Hayes at Cole, 387-3859) in the Haight still has an authentic hippie vibe — serving up some cheap substantial food as well. Great for post-Park resuscitation.

Mission poets have long frequented **La Boheme** (3318 24th St. at Mission, 643-0481), an airy open room, with local art on the walls and good bulletin boards with notices of apartment shares, etc.

COMING DOWN • Shortcut to Infamy • Some of the City's most famous denizens have built a career upon excessive alcohol intake—where would Kerouac be without years perched on barstools? Banish the thought. Following is a sample of some non-foo-foo drinking establishments (hint: most are better on weeknights).

North Beach's best-known litbars are within stumbling distance of City Lights: **Spec's** (12 Adler at Broadway, 421-4112) is full of cranky poets on any given night—the place is crammed full of weird old memorabilia, including some of the customers. Be a poet or just look like one parked under a large portrait of James Joyce on the balcony upstairs at **Vesuvio** (255 Columbus at Broadway, 362-3370). Key seating is upstairs by the front window at sunset when the Broadway lights come on—pints of Anchor Steam are an essential part of the total experience!

When in the Mission, fall off your barstool at the **Uptown** (200 Capp at 17th St., 861-8231) or the **Dovre Club** (1498 Valencia at 26th St., 285-4169). Poet David West recommends visiting the **Wild Side West** (424 Cortland at Wool St., 647-3099) on a weeknight—he says be sure to check out the toilet collection in the backyard.

San Francisco is home to several micro-breweries, where beer is brewed on the premises and changes seasonally. Check out the **San Francisco Brewing Company** (155 Columbus at Kearny, 434-3344) in North Beach, with its turn-of-the century interior. Babyface Nelson was nailed here by the Feds long before it was a microbrewery.

If you really feel like doing something different, drinking at **Diva's** (1081 Post at Polk, 928-6006) is like being in a John Waters movie. Also recommended is the **Club Charleston** (10 6th St. at Market, 431-0544) for cheap cocktails in a classic dive bar.

The Edinburgh Castle (950 Geary, 885-4074) is always good for a pint of lager, and a heap of fish and chips wrapped in traditional newspaper from around the corner at **The Old Chelsea** (932 Larkin, 474-5015).

GOING OUT

Spoken Word • Poetry readings constitute one of the best entertainment values in the City because they're free. Maybe you'll even get to participate in a poets' brawl. You might even get to hear some great writing and/or profoundly lame haikus. Each reading has its own distinct flavor and characteristics. All have featured readers in addition to open mikes, get there early if you'd like to participate. For even more readings, check out the Spoken Word listings in the free weeklies or pick up Poetry Flash, a free monthly poetry info source distributed at independent literary bookstores. Always call first to make sure the readings are still happening.

MONDAY
    Celebration of the Word - Featured readers at 7 p.m.

followed by an open mic. - **Notes from the Underground Café** (2399 Van Ness at Green, 775-7638)

Poetry Nitro - Featured reader followed by an open mic. Every Monday. Sign up 7:30, reading 8-10 p.m. at **Café de la Paz** (1600 Shattuck at Cedar, Berkeley, 510-843-0664)

TUESDAY

Word Dancing - all open reading. Tuesdays, from 7-9 p.m. - **Andalusia Café**, (1209 Sutter at Polk, 928-8904)

WEDNESDAY

Spoken Word Salon – Bring your laundry. Featured reader plus open. 8 p.m. **Brainwash Café & Laundromat** (1122 Folsom at 8th St., 437-2363)

Sacred Grounds – Long-running open reading. 7 p.m. - **Sacred Grounds** (2095 Hayes at Masonic, 387-3859)

Bezerkley Slam – The Berkeley slam. Sign up at 8 p.m., show from 8:30-11 p.m. $5, all ages before 9 p.m., 21+ after. - **Starry Plough** (3101 Shattuck at Prince, Berkeley, 510-841-2082)

Poetry in the Café – Featured readers and open mike. $2-5 donation requested. - **La Pena Cultural Center** (3105 Shattuck at Prince, Berkeley, 510-849-2568)

THURSDAY

Where Words Sustain Us - The Oakland slam - Sign up at 7:30, show 8 p.m. Open mic follows at 10 p.m. $5. **Mambo** (1803 Webster, Oakland, 510-596-8909)

FRIDAY

Café International - Featured reader at 8 p.m. followed by open mic. **Café International** (508 Haight at Fillmore, 474-6159)

Yakety Yak – Open reading 7:30 p.m. **Yakety Yak**

Coffeehouse (679 Sutter at Taylor, 351-2090)

SUNDAY

Second Sundays – Second Sunday of every month, San Francisco slam. Sign up at 7:30 p.m., show from 8-11 p.m. $5 before 9 p.m., $8 after, 21+ only. **Justice League** (628 Divisadero at Hayes, 289-2038)

Sweetie's Open Mic - Featured reader followed by open mike. Every Sunday at 7:30 p.m., 21 and over - **Sweetie's** (475 Francisco at Powell, 433-2343)

MOVIES, THEATER, DANCE & PERFORMANCE

MOVIES

There are dozens of movies showing at any given moment in this town. Here are a few venues for checking out the silver screen.

The Roxie (3117 16th St. at Valencia, 863-1087) and **Red Vic** (1727 Haight at Cole, 668-3994) have new independent films as well as repertory showings. As does **The Castro** (429 Castro at Market, 621-6120), one of San Francisco's grandest movie theaters, which even has a guy playing the Mighty Wurlitzer. The orchestra pit in the front of the theater swallows the Wurlitzer and guy.

The Kabuki (Post at Fillmore, 931-9800) movie theaters have half-price matinees all afternoon — 8 different screens, such a choice.

SF Cinematheque (822-2885, www.sfcinematheque.org) is in its 40th season of presenting experimental and non-commercial films at majorly affordable prices. Screenings are usually Sunday evenings at the **SF Art Institute** (800

Chestnut at Jones) or Thursday evenings at the **Yerba Buena Center for the Arts** (701 Mission at 3rd St., 978-2787).

ATA also known as **Artists Television Access** (992 Valencia at 21st St., 824-3890) screens underground videos and films, as well as offering workshops and renting video editing equipment to aspiring filmmakers.

THEATER, DANCE & PERFORMANCE

TIX, a.k.a. **Tix Bay Area Half Price Ticket Booth** (Union Square, 333 Post at Stockton, 433-7827) has half-price tickets for that evening's mainstream and alternative theater performances. Stop by and see what's available.

Ft. Mason (Marina at Buchanan) is home to both the **Magic Theater** (441-8822) and the **Cowell Theater** (441-3400), call for programming details.

LunaSea (2940 16th St. at South Van Ness, 2nd floor, 863-2989) features women-only cabaret, performance art, readings, and more.

The Marsh (1062 Valencia at 22nd St., 826-5750) hosts solo performers performing works in progress and finished works as well on Monday nights and weekends.

Intersection for the Arts (446 Valencia at 15th St., 626-2787) is a community-oriented space, complete with art gallery and theater. Programs include drama, dance, readings and writing workshops.

Cellspace (2050 Bryant, 648-7562) is an awesome theater space that features music and theater performances, spoken word events, and more. Always a great scene, lots of alternative programming you won't find elsewhere.

Theater Rhinoceros (2940 16th St., 861-5079) produces more than 5 shows every year, all about queer lives, issues, thoughts, and feelings.

Exit Theater (156 Eddy, 673-3847) hosts the SF Fringe Festival and Theater of the Absurd among other productions.

WHERE TO HAVE A
POETIC EXPERIENCE

While inspiration lurks everywhere and anywhere in this town, here are a few places that have a built-in appreciation factor — great for contemplation and composition. May your muse always broadcast loud and clear.

Ocean Beach (at the end of Golden Gate Park and the Great Highway) is huge and accessible for long windswept walks, peering into the vastness of ocean and air — always a relief after an overdose of humanity.

Near Ocean Beach are the ruins of **Sutro Baths** — all that remains of a once thriving civic wonder from the turn of the last century — San Francisco's own reminder of past glory and fallen civilization. Wander among the ruins and ponder. (Near Cliff House & end of Geary)

Beyond the throngs and hordes of Fisherman's Wharf is a quiet pier located behind Scoma's restaurant (Pier 47,

Fisherman's Wharf) — perfect for that *Sittin' on the Dock of the Bay* kind of mood, a place to watch sailboats, harbor seals, Alcatraz, the Golden Gate bridge, and all of that corny stuff. **Crissy Field** (GGNRA Presidio entrance, end of Marina Blvd.) also offers great views and a lovely windswept walk along the edge of the bay by the Golden Gate Bridge.

Nearby at the end of the Fisherman's Wharf area is **Aquatic Park** (Beach & Hyde), where on weekends drummers drum and humans lie around like seals basking in the sunshine.

For quiet contemplation near the Haight, the **Strybing Arboretum** (Lincoln at 9th St., 661-1316) is a botanical garden in Golden Gate Park that can provide many hours of thoughtful solace. The humid Conservatory (Arguello at Fulton) is filled with strange tropical plants. There's even a small herd of buffalo who are always looking for company. Golden Gate Park is full of amazing discoveries.

Jack Early Park (Grant at Chestnut) is a tiny promontory with a sweeping view of the Bay, perfect for solitude or a secret rendezvous.

Climb any hill — Telegraph, Russian, Nob, Potrero, Twin Peaks, Bernal Heights, 17th Street, wherever — and look at the view when you catch your breath.

WHERE'S THE PARTY?
BY YOLANDA MONTIJO

When we're not waiting to die, working, hunting for a parking spot or a safe place to lock our bikes, or trying to agree on where to meet for dinner, San Franciscans love to party. Especially free parties. Year round, rain or shine, morning fog or evening fog, San Franciscans and friends love to take to the streets and get busy. The following is a list of mostly annual, mostly free, big San Francisco parties.

Call the listed numbers for directions or more information, or check out the very comprehensive San Francisco Visitors Bureau site at www.sfvisitor.org (complete with visitor maps, online yellow pages for SF and a full schedule of almost every cultural event in the city.) For a more opinionated view of what's going on around town, try the weekly rags, the *SF Bay Guardian* or *SF Weekly*, or check out www.citysearch.com.

JANUARY

Chinese New Year Parade and Celebration

Near the end of January

Chinatown

Information: 982-3000; www.chinese parade.com

Snake, horse, monkey, rat... what year is it again? Fabulous fabulous fabulous. The parade usually starts in the early evening at Market and 2nd St. and goes to Columbus. Get there as early as possible.

MARCH

San Francisco International Asian American Film Festival

AMC Kabuki Theatres and other venues

Information: 863-0814

Documentaries, shorts, experimental films and videos from North America, the Pacific and the greater Asian Diaspora.

St. Patrick's Day Parade

March 12

2nd St. and Market to Civic Center

Information: 731-0924

Get green the old-fashioned way. This is one of San Francisco's largest annual parades. Begins in the afternoon, at 2nd and Market St. and ends at City Hall in the Civic Center area.

APRIL

St. Stupid's Day Parade

April Fools Day

Join the First Church of the Last Laugh and the Cacophony Society in a parade through the Financial District to Washington Square Park promoting zaniness and the importance of being silly. Always a hoot.

Cherry Blossom Festival
Japantown
Information: 563-2313
Japantown's party is generally two weekends of performances, crafts, amazing food, martial arts exhibitions, plus a parade from Civic Center to Fillmore.

San Francisco International Film Festival
Castro Theatre and other venues
Information: 561-5000
The best way to see the world without leaving the city. A favorite film feast for many, this truly international film festival usually showcases over 100 films from as many as 30 different countries

MAY
Cinco de Mayo
May 5
Mission District
Information: 826-1401
Mexico's Independence day. A hot and gorgeous festival, jam packed with mariachis, food, arts, crafts and a parade down Mission from 24th St. to 14th St.

Carnaval
Near the end of May
Mission District
Information: 826-1401
Mardi Gras the San Francisco way. A big, fun, sweaty San Francisco mass party and parade you will not want to miss. The parade generally goes from 24th and Bryant to Harrison.

Bay to Breakers
Third Sunday in May

Information:
Run 7.6 miles from the Bay to Ocean Beach with tens of thousands of other costumed sweaty marathoners.

JUNE

Haight Street Fair

Haight St.
Information: 661-8025
Haight St. in the summer. Enough said. Live bands, barbecues, goods, and everything edible and smokeable imaginable. The kids come out for this one. Wear your tie-dye.

San Francisco Lesbian/Gay/Bisexual/Transgender Pride Celebration Parade

Third Sunday in June
Embarcadero to Civic Center
Information: 864-FREE
Say it loud, say it proud. The mother of Gay Pride parades. San Francisco's very fabulous annual celebration of lesbian and gay pride culminates with a festive parade from the Embarcadero to Civic Center.

San Francisco International Lesbian and Gay Film Festival

Castro Theatre and other venues
Information: 703-8663
If you've come for the Gay Pride parade, then don't miss the film festival. The largest and oldest event of its kind in the world, this festival features hundreds of flicks from around the globe.

Juneteenth Celebration

Information: 440-5863

Great, obviously annual celebration of African American culture.

Fiesta Filipina
Civic Center Plaza
Information: 989-0288
The largest Bay Area Filipino festival featuring Filipino cuisine, entertainment, arts and crafts and carnival rides.

North Beach Festival
Grant Ave. and Green St.
Information: 989-6426
Who doesn't love North Beach? Though North Beach is generally its own yearlong party, this is the festival to come to see it all happening at once. Get caffeinated, get drunk, and check out the neighborhood as it celebrates itself in true Italian/bohemian style.

Summer Stages
All month
701 Mission St.
San Francisco
Information: 978-ARTS
A free, repeat free, great and wildly diverse outdoor performance series running through October at Yerba Buena Gardens, in the heart of downtown. A great opportunity to see hot and funky Bay Area musicians, poets and writers, with a focus on rising talent. Call for performance schedules and dates.

JULY
Fourth of July Waterfront Festival
July 4
Fisherman's Wharf

Information: 705-5500
The annual July 4th waterfront party. If you can't make it to the waterfront, find a roof somewhere and gaze heavenward at the awesome fireworks show; always just as good as being there. Live entertainment, food, and buyable goods. Remember: it's nighttime and by the bay, so dress warmly.

Books By the Bay
Pier 32, The Embarcadero
Information: 561-7686
Get close to the bay and down with the best of the Bay Area's bookstores at this outdoor book fair. Readings, signings, children's area, and good food. If the sun's out, whatever you do, don't your forget your hat or umbrella.

SF Mime Troupe in the Park
July 4 through the summer at various locations
They don't do mime. For more than thirty years, this esteemed crew has put on original musical dramas with a leftist political bent in Bay Area parks for free. Very fun, very San Francisco.

SEPTEMBER
Burning Man
Labor Day Weekend in Nevada
863-5263, www.burningman.com
Join 30,000 of your closest friends in the dusty free-for-all moveable city known as Burning Man. It's expensive but if you don't have the money, volunteer to work at it...

Folsom Street Fair
Near the end of the month
Folsom St.
Information: 861-3247

The most popular and legendary of San Francisco's street fairs and the place to meet the truly underground. A free-for-all parade unto itself. Skin everywhere. See or buy S&M, bondage gear or leather goods of all kinds. Live bands, food, get spanked for charity.

San Francisco Open Studios

Various locations
Information: 861-9838
Though you can't get inside the head of your favorite artist, or many artists for that matter, at least you can get inside their studios. Open Studios gives you the chance to wander through a vast variety of artist studios, big and small, in every sense of the world, and get up close and personal with the artists themselves. And should you fall in love with their work on the spot, there's always the chance you can bargain with them. This is a free market country after all.

San Francisco Blues Festival

Great Meadow at Fort Mason
Information: 979-5588
The oldest blues festival in America with some of the best blues musicians in the world.

San Francisco Fringe Festival

Exit Theatre/various downtown venues
Information: 673-3847
Still putting the heat in theatre, the Fringe Festival works hard to remind us of what theatre can and should be. A non-juried, non-censored marathon of over 200 performances by more than 50 theater companies, this festival takes place at the Exit Theatre, in the heart of the fringe tenderloin and the city, and other smaller theatre spaces around the city. Always a worthy cause.

How Berkeley Can You Be? Parade

Usually the last weekend in September

Shattuck Ave, Berkeley

Artcars, naked people, and lots more stuff celebrating the politically-correct People's Republic of Berkeley.

OCTOBER

Castro Street Fair

Usually the first of the month

Castro St.

Information: 467-3354

Like North Beach, the Castro is always a fair. The pageantry is always spectacular: Hieronymous Bosch meets Tom of Finland.

San Francisco Jazz Festival

Monthlong

Various locations

Information: 788-7353

During the beatnik '50s, San Francisco was legendary for its jazz culture, and now it's home to one of the biggest and best jazz festivals anywhere. Local, national and international jazz artists make hot all over the city. Call or check out the weeklies for listings.

Halloween San Francisco

10/31

Castro

There's the Castro and then there's Halloween in the Castro. The unofficial and real San Francisco Halloween party. While the rest of the city is at the Civic Center, catch any public transportation to the Castro and be prepared to see anything. This event is never advertised.

NOVEMBER
Film Arts Festival of Independent Cinema
Castro and Roxie Theaters
Information: 552-8760
Hundreds of films by local artists showcase the real underground and diversity of San Francisco and Northern California.

DECEMBER
New Year's Eve
Celebrate anywhere.

ONGOING
Critical Mass
last Friday of every month, meet at 5 p.m. at Market & Embarcadero
Grab a bike and join fellow pedal revolutionaries at the foot of Market Street for a ride from here to wherever, clogging up automotive traffic and promoting non-polluting alternative transportation.

FREE & CHEAP ENTERTAINMENT

Outdoor Fun & Sports • The fact that the weather tends to be eternally Spring-like lends itself to activities in the Great Outdoors. While destinations like Yosemite, Big Sur, Point Reyes, and Mt. Tamalpais are within spitting distance, here are a few that are a tad closer to home.

For a great day trip of outdoor adventure, take the **Ferry to Angel Island** (435-2131) for a picnic and hike. Weekends only. Or just hop a ferry to Sausalito or Oakland any day of the week.

During summer weekends through October, the SF **Shakespeare Festival** (422-2222) presents free Shakespeare plays in Golden Gate Park.

During the summer months, the **Stern Grove Festival** (252-6252, www.sterngrove.org) presents free programs at Golden Gate Park's Stern Grove by notables like the Preservation Hall Jazz Band; the SF Ballet, the SF Opera, and more. Bring a blanket and a picnic.

Grab your clubs and play a few holes at a San Francisco public Golf Course: Harding Park, Lincoln Park, Sharp Park, Fleming and Golden Gate Park. Call for info. (753-7249, or for reservations 750-4653).

Tennis, anyone? SF also has public tennis courts. Call 753-7100 for info.

Go for a swim or take lessons in any of SF's nine public swimming pools. 831-2700 for info.

The San Francisco Zoo (Sloat at 45th Ave., 753-7080) is free the first Wednesday of every month—visit the animals with some kids for a real thrill.

Free Walking Tours • Dozens of free walking tours are conducted every month by City Guides, a volunteer service of Friends of the San Francisco Public Library. Most walks take about an hour and a half. Tours are available for almost every neighborhood in the City, including Chinatown, North Beach, Pacific Heights mansions, and a whole bunch more. Call 557-4266 for detailed information, including time schedules and starting points.

• The following MUSEUMS are FREE the first Wednesday of every month:

Exploratorium. A hands-on science museum that's uniquely amazing. (Lyon at Marina, 561-0360)

Steinhart Aquarium. Home of the godlike Fish Roundabout and more. Not to be missed. (Golden Gate Park, 750-7145)

DeYoung Museum. Closed for remodeling, but check it out when it re-opens in a new state-of-the-art facility in 2005. Features art, changing exhibits. Also free the first Saturday of every month from 10 a.m. till noon. $2 discount for Muni or Fastpass holders. (Golden Gate Park, 75 Tea Garden Drive, 750-3600)

San Francisco Museum of Modern Art is free the first TUESDAY of every month, and offers reduced admission on Thursday evenings after 5 p.m. when it's open till 9. Also free admission for the last 45 minutes of every day it's open. (151 Third St. at Howard, www.sfmo.org, 357-4000)

Cartoon Art Museum is pay-what-you-can the first TUESDAY of every month. Everything from Krazy Kat to R. Crumb as long as it's cartoons, comics or comix. (655 Mission at Third St., CAR-TOON; www.cartoonart.org, 227-8666)

Weird Museums

Feel like going for a drive? Visit the **Burlingame Museum of Pez Memorabilia** (214 California Dr., Burlingame, 650-347-2301, Free, Tues.-Sat. 10 a.m.-6 p.m.) where gazillions of Pez dispensers are on display.

Here in SF, visit the **Golden Gate Railroad Museum** (Hunters Point Naval Shipyard, end of Evans St., 822-8728, Sat./Sun. 10 a.m.-5p.m., adults $5, kids/seniors $2) where you can get up close and personal with steam trains and diesel locomotives. In fact, you can even make advance reservations to drive a steam engine (Toot!Toot!) yourself ($300/hour).

Also fabulous is the **Sanitary Landfill Sculpture Garden** (401 Tunnel Ave., free monthly tours by appointment only, 330-1415), a 3-acre hilltop sculpture garden filled with artwork made of recycled trash by a series of artists-in-residence.

The **Historic Nike Missile Museum** (Marin Headlands,

331-1453, www.nikemissile.net, free, call for hours and info) is at the site of a Cold War nightmare: visit the ICBM site which was to deliver nuclear warheads to the USSR. War is bad. Never forget.

More Fun

Everybody has different ideas about what's fun, but here are some tried and true suggestions.

Visit the **Basic Brown Bear Factory** (444 DeHaro at Mariposa, 626-0781) and see teddy bears being made.

Check out **Golden Gate Fortune Cookie Company** (56 Ross Alley at Jackson, 781-3956) and see fortune cookies being made (how do they get those little pieces of paper in there?)

Take a tour of the **Anchor Steam Brewing Company** (1705 Mariposa at DeHaro, 863-8350), available by appointment only. Book 3-4 weeks in advance. The tasting room awaits at the end of the tour.

The **Scharffen Berger Chocolate Factory** (914 Heinz Ave., Berkeley, 510-981-4050) offers free 1-hour tours of their unique, upscale chocolate factory where they roast their own cocoa beans. Call for reservations.

The **Jelly Belly Candy Co.** (Fairfield, 800-522-3267, call for directions and info) is located about an hour away by car: it's a real working jelly bean factory so be sure to go on a weekday when they're cranking out the candy.

Dreyer's Grand Ice Cream Factory (Union City, 510-477-3271) is also located about an hour from SF, tour reservations are required and get booked up fast so be sure to call ahead.

The **San Francisco Ballet** (Opera House, 401 Van Ness at Grove, 865-2000, www.sfballet.org), when in season, sells balcony seats for $9 each — whatta deal for symphonic music, great dance, terrific costumes, and excellent buns!

American Conservatory Theater (ACT) (405 Geary, 749-2228) has cheap tickets ($8, second balcony) to preveiw nights - live theater less than a first-run movie.

The venerable **Roxie Cinema** (3117 16th St. near Valencia, 863-1087) offers a pass (5 movies/$22) good for one year, must be used by only one person, and can't be used for festivals.

Ride the **cable cars** late at night when they're almost empty (they run till midnight). Total fun riding on the outside singing show tunes in the wind. Tell the conductor you can't find your Fastpass—he might let you ride for free. Then again, he might kick you off immediately if you don't have your money ready. Oops! The **vintage streetcars** that run on Market Street are also fun - my favorite is the open-air one that looks like a boat.

Cool Music at Church: Jazz with prayers at the **Church of John Coltrane** (934 Gough at Turk, 673-3572). **Glide Memorial** (434 Ellis at Taylor, 674-6000) has an uplifting gospel choir.

Almost Free Bus Tours: Certain MUNI routes cut all the way across San Francisco and if you secure a window seat, you can experience a mighty fine San Francisco tour for $1, roundtrip with transfer. Recommended is the 22 Fillmore line rolling from the Marina waterfront through Pacific Heights, the Mission, Potrero Hill and beyond, all the way to Third Street. The 29 Sunset goes out to Baker Beach and offers some great views, as does the 39 Corbett. Buy a MUNI map at most corner grocery stores.

KID FRIENDLY SF

While plenty of folks move out to Petaluma or Pleasanton or wherever once they have kids, others have chosen to stay in the city because even if they don't get to hang out as much at the Sacrifice or stay out late at the Make-out Room, well, they're nearby if you wanted to.

RESOURCES

Natural Resources (1301 Castro St. near 24th St., 550-2611) This well-informed storefront operation in Noe Valley sells practical baby items like books, breast pumps, and baby slings, and also offers classes in natural childbirth and labor coaching. An informative library of books is next to a comfortable couch where you can read up on what the alternative experts have to say about childbirth and parenting. Natural Resources also offers community open listings for babysitters and labor coaches.

Perinatal Education and Lactation Center at California Pacific Medical Center (3698 California St. near Webster, 1st floor, 346-BABY) You don't need health insurance, and it doesn't matter where you gave birth to participate in CPMC's drop-in new mothers group.

Parents Place (3272 California St., 563-1041) An enormous variety of programs for parents and kids (newborn through teens), including support groups, workshops, counseling, a drop-in play area, and parenting library. If you need sound advice or support with a specific situation ("My child refuses to eat anything except spaghetti"), call their Warm Line, 931-WARM...within 24 hours a licensed child therapist will call you back.

Telephone Aid in Living with Kids (TALK) Line (757 Waller St., 441-KIDS) A 24-hour crisis line for parents - don't hit your kids, don't freak out, call these people instead and speak with a trained counselor who can help you cope with your situation. The TALK Line also sponsors private counseling services on a sliding scale, and parenting skills workshops including single parents, parents of adolescents, and mother and infants groups. All are on-going, and are offered at no charge.

San Francisco Public Libraries: Both the Main Library and the branches offer activities for all ages. Weekly programs are held for infants to teenagers.

City College Department of Child Development and Family Studies: For more than 20 years, City College has offered 'Child Observation' classes for parents. A step beyond playgroups, special sites located all over San Francisco host environments with age-appropriate toys and climbing structures for two-and-a-half hour sessions led by a certified instructor. Parents also learn about age-appropriate topics like health and safety, sleep patterns, and toilet training. Classes meet once a week and are divided into three age groups: newborn-7 months, 8-14 months, and 15+ months. These are all free non-credit classes. Parents register at the site. For information about times and locations, call 561-1921.

Children's Council of San Francisco (243-0111) Once maternity leave is over and it's time to go back to work, where will the little one go? A resource and referral line for parents seeking licensed daycare providers is offered by the Children's Council of San Francisco.

If you're interesting in adopting a child with minimal expense, check out the **SF Child Project** (1-800-732-4453). They provide guidance and support throughout the process.

If you're interested in becoming a foster parent, call **SF Human Services** (557-6284). There's a great need in the Bay Area for foster families to help local kids.

Precita Eyes Mural Project (348 Precita, 285-2311) offers low-cost drop-in art classes almost daily for kids. **Mission Cultural Center** (2868 Mission at 25th St., 821-1155) offers free capoeira classes for kids, and a low-cost after-school program, too. **826 Valencia** (826 Valencia, 642-5905) has free tutoring for high school kids, and **Youth Speaks** (2169 Folsom, 255-9035) offers free poetry, performance, and writing workshops for high schoolers. **SF Rec & Parks Dept.** has swimming lessons for children, play programs for preschoolers, after-school sports and arts programs for bigger kids, and really great daycamp programs during the summer. Look in the SF phone book, in the SF gov't pages, under Rec & Parks.

ENTERTAINMENT

The **Coyote Point Museum** (1651 Coyote Point Dr., San Mateo, 650-342-7755) located by the Bay about 20 minutes south of the city is an environmental learning center and museum featuring many live animals and nature exhibits. If you purchase an annual membership here ($55 for a family membership), you get free admission to the awesome **Academy of Sciences** in Golden Gate Park AKA the dinosaur museum: don't miss the fish roundabout in the aquarium; the astounding **Exploratorium** (Marina Blvd. and Lyon, 561-0360) - a hands-on science museum with interactive, participatory exhibits; and the **SF Zoo** (Sloat Blvd. and 46th Ave.), many acres and many animals out by the ocean. One of the best deals in town! All of these museums offer summer camps for kids, too.

The always-free **Randall Museum** (Roosevelt Way and 14th St., 554-9600) has a bunch of science exhibits (love the see-through active beehive) and some cute little live animals. They also offer low-cost craft and science workshops for kids on Saturdays.

Yerba Buena Gardens offers kids a **carousel**, a **skating rink** and **bowling alley** (750 Folsom, 777-3727), and **Zeum** (221 4th St., 777-2800) - a participatory art museum for ages 6 and up, and is a MUCH better scene than the inanely commercial, overpriced **Metreon**. ODC performs *The Velveteen Rabbit*, an hour-long modern dance piece for kids, every holiday season at the **Yerba Buena Theater**, tickets are around $10. It's a good alternative to the SF Ballet's *Nutcracker.*

If you must take your kid to *The Nutcracker*, get your tickets at half-price with a free **ArtsCard** (974-5554, www.yabayarca.org), which also gets the child cardholder reduced prices at many museums, plays and other performances (SF Opera, too!) as well as Marin's **Bay Area Discovery Museum** (Fort Baker, Sausalito, 487-4398) - a fun place with participatory exhibits and arts and crafts programs for little kids that can be slightly expensive otherwise.

My all-time favorite place for kids under 10 is Oakland's **Children's Fairyland** (on the northern side of Lake Merritt at Grand Ave. and Bellevue, 510-238-6876). An inspiration to Walt Disney in the '50s before Disneyland, it's been recently renovated and is as cool as ever. The old-time puppet show three times a day with deftly handled marionettes is an endless source of amazement. Rides, exhibits, a few live animals, picnic tables, and more. You can't come here if you don't have a kid with you.

Some neighborhood Rec & Park rec centers, like Moscone on Chestnut St. in the Marina, have ongoing free or low-cost sports, art, programs for kids of all ages. Call around to see what's offered. Look in the phone inder San

Francisco Rec & Park.

For more kid-friendly ideas and Bay Area resources, check out **www.gokid.org** online.

**ART ATTACK
BY
MARY FITZGERALD**

If your idea of a great art gallery is one offering nubile bronze women or a painting that matches your couch, stick to the Fisherman's Wharf or Union Square galleries. However, if you wanna see what SF artists are up to lately in terms of being profound, cutting edge and maybe even trendy, pick a neighborhood and have a fun afternoon.

Warning: artists and gallery directors lead complicated lives. Call before visiting to confirm the hours, the show, or even if the gallery still exists.

PUBLICATIONS

Check current listings in the *SF Weekly* or *Bay Guardian* (includes opening reception times and a brief Critic's Choice review) or the *Wave* (a local free monthly with prominent art listings and a full page interview with a local artist.)

There's also *SF Arts Monthly* and *Artweek* (a monthly with reviews of selected shows from last month). Once you get to a gallery look around for postcards and gallery guides. On the internet, visit www.SFArts.org.

LOWER POTRERO HILL

California College of Arts: Crafts-Logan Galleries and Carol Weisel Hall (111 8th St., 551-9210) An entrance like a clean, moderne hotel lobby. Check out the student body and their hairstyles. Logan Galleries to the left, C.W. Hall straight ahead past the security guard who may want you to sign in.

Logan Galleries present impressive group shows of U.S. and European artists, with an ironic, ultra-contemporary twist. Recent themes have been Rock and Roll and "slapstick in contemporary art." Slick catalogs are sometimes available for a donation of $5. Arts patron Phyllis Wattis (God rest her soul) dumped a lot of dough into this well-managed space.

Carol Weisel Hall is much more informal. Sometimes student work is on the walls or a participatory installation by a "real" artist. Spy on attentive students in their immaculate studios. Have a tuna with chopped pecans salad at the pricey, fab cafe before you go. Lots of chrome and glass. This art school is nothing like the dusty, run-down one I attended.

Gallery 16 (1616 16th St., 626-7495) Promotes Digital prints, but not exclusively. Located on the 3rd floor of one of SF's few brick buildings. Partners with their neighbor Urban Digital Color in the production of artists books and multiples. Cool stuff with a 2-D cyber-photo bent, iconography like David Bowie or desert landscapes as seen from the windows of a rented Buick.

San Francisco Center for the Book (300 De Haro at

16th St., 565-0545) A great space for an intriguing art world niche - handmade artists' books. The mezzanine gallery showcases book art ranging from xeroxed zines to one-of-a-kind gems. Pieces displayed focus more on sculptural or painterly qualities than beautiful typesetting. Classes in letterset printing and bookbinding are offered in their bright studio.

Ambersand International Arts (1001 Tennessee at 20th St., 285-0170) Hop over the 280 freeway to Dogpatch. This gallery is housed in one of the thousands of live/work units that have been built recently. The work I saw looked very macho Ab/Ex. You know, process and material dictating the form. Thickly applied paintings and sculpture hewn from trees. There's a cute dog in residence, too.

NORTHEAST MISSION

Southern Exposure (401 Alabama St., 863-2141) Located in Project Artaud, the city's oldest and coolest artists live/work space, SoEx's main gallery boasts the largest exhibition wall at 56 feet long x 20 feet high. Count on seeing lively works about the human condition. Topics covered have been bloodshed in suburbia, sex lives of the disabled, and skateboarding.

Culture Cache (1800 Bryant St. #104 at 17th St., 626-7776) A corner live/work space with windows on two sides allows peeking at the show even when the gallery is closed. The "mission school" is hot right now and they've got it covered. Lurid graffiti-style paintings delivered on wood panels or thrift store frames. Urban landscapes and its outcasts in candy colors. You might even see the director's baby take her first steps on the polished floors.

Peres Project (1800 Bryant St. #210 at 17th St., 861-2692) Get buzzed in and make your way past the warehouse-chic residences in this live/work building to the 2nd floor.

Project director Javier will greet you with a chihuahua under his arm. He shows the up-and-coming international artists seen in the Whitney Biennial or the Venice Bieniale. The inaugural show of videos was mesmerizing: rural and urban architecture either rushing or floating by, some images shot upside down, all with a rock and roll soundtrack.

INNER MISSION

Pond (214 Valencia St., 437-9151) Billing itself as "a place for art, activism and ideas," Pond is a small but big-hearted space on a crummy block. It deals with art that talks about food via intestinal shapes molded on the wall. It supplies pens so viewers can join in the cause. It participated in Ladyfest by mounting a show of comix art by women including Dame Darcy and bitter pie.

Jack Hanley Gallery (395 Valencia St., 522-1623) Why this gallery moved from its former downtown home, I don't know. Maybe to be closer to the **Lady Luck Candle Shop** (311 Valencia). It has retained its big pricetags and girl with attitude behind desk, and shows contemporary works like the junior high notebook doodles done ad nauseam on 9 foot reams of paper. Like the minimal architectural renderings done with an exacto knife. Get a Raymond Pettibone drawing silkscreened on a T-shirt for 10 bucks.

Intersection for the Arts (446 Valencia, 626-ARTS) Known for its theatre and spoken word programs, this non-profit also hosts politically charged visual art exhibits upstairs. Look for the stairway to the left inside the entrance, or behind the stage. In an effort to give everyone a chance to be represented, the shows can be about extraordinarily specific groups, like gay African Americans who have lost their rent-controlled apartments. Maybe their funding depends on it. There's a poster from the 1985 Halloween show I was in hanging up near the bathroom.

The Lab (2948 16th St. at Capp, 864-8855) The gallery has a large space in a building the once housed many labor union offices -there are contemporary murals (including one by Barry McGee) honoring them in the main lobby. This non-profit has been around for a while and tends to show art that looks like it just got out of bed. I guess the artists are more concerned with making a statement than with neatness or production values. Site specific installations involving piles of clutter or film loops predominate. Start your West Coast Artists collection at their annual silent auction fundraiser.

Glama-rama (417 So. Van Ness Ave. at 15th St., 861-4526) Two pink 6 foot tall stuffed toy poodles sit in the window of this beauty parlor/art gallery. It's really funky and there's that toxic hair dye smell. Art by the salon's clients and their pals is displayed on the upper portion of the 15 foot high walls. If the show up there doesn't work for you, check out each stylist's found-object custom-made station. It's like a cross between Rube Goldberg and John Waters! Needless to everybody there has great hair, too.

THE MISSION

Spanganga (3376 19th St., 821-1102, www.spanganga.org) A lot of interesting things happen at this gallery. Once I was looking at a quilt made out of bras and a troupe of men in white jumpsuits dusted with black powder marched out of the back room. The summer show was called "I Hate Being a Girl." The street number was applied over the front entrance with a large brush and drippy black paint, proclaiming itself a gallery that doesn't care what you think of it.

Paxton Gate (824 Valencia, 824-1872) A beautiful garden store for goths and kinky scientists. There's a small back room showcasing art that looks good with their merchandise: the same incredible rusted metals, taxidermied creatures, and dried flora and fauna.

Artists Television Access (992 Valencia, 824-3890) ATA is so cool. It's mostly a screening room for its Saturday night Other Cinema. Low-cost classes in video production are offered, too. Sometimes they move the theater seats and hang art. Most times there are great installations in the front windows dealing with issues like high rents or porno or being an angry artist. This place is punk rock to its core.

a.o.v. (3328 22nd St., 431-8341) is a teeny but tidy space. Last spring there was an installation involving sand bags slung over the door, used tea bags on the floor and tiny black nails hammered into the walls. It was all very calmly and thoughtfully arranged. The shows don't change very often, but the director wears suits and sits behind a very important-looking desk so I imagine there is more good stuff to come.

Lola Gallery (2519 Mission, 401-6800) Lots of promise for this new gallery (with built-in bar!) where the shows feature a *lot* of artists working in *every* media. The inaugural show's theme of "Symmetry" was derived from 2002 being the only palindromic year in this century. "She's Crafty" celebrated female ingenuity and the interplay between Art and Craft. I visited during installation of an exhibition called "Riding the Range." Bales of hay were being dragged up the staircase in preparation for a mock cowboy shoot-out. Yee-Haa!

Mission Cultural Center For Latino Arts (2868 Mission, 821-115) Come to the twilight Day of the Dead procession on November 1st, then visit the room-sized altars installed in the large upstairs gallery. Opulent tributes to the dearly departed are decorated lavishly with family photos, flowers, paintings ,beaded crucifixes, and psychedelic

Virgins of Guadalupe. I only wish the frigid Irish Catholic church of my youth had been half this joyful. The center offers exhibitions, classes and entertainment year-round.

Balazo/Mission Badlands Gallery (2811 Mission, 920-0896) Underground in spirit, but located on the top floor of the building that houses Western Dental and Frida's Pizza, it's worth the search just to see the mural by Mats!? in the "Event Room." There have been shows about Satanism and a show of Italian punk posters from the '80s. "Live Nude Boxes" is a new quarterly event where women present work about breaking free from repressive cultural expectations. Opening and closing parties feature performances and music.

Galleria de la Raza (2857 24th St., 826-8009) Thirty-one years old and deep in the heart of the Mission, the gallery was started by Chicano rights activists as a place for art that address the experiences of Latino/as. Recent shows include "Viology/ Cultures of Violence" and "Substance of Choice 19 Emerging Artists." Films and talks also support the theme of the shows. **Studio 24**, the neighboring boutique, helps support gallery programs with the sale of fun decorative objects from Mexico: floral-patterned shopping bags, postcards, Day of the Dead ceramics, and mugs shaped like the head of Santos, the silver-masked wrestling legend.

Balmy Alley (off 24th between Folsom and Harrison) Every wall, fence and garage door of this sunny block long alley is covered with murals in rich, saturated color. It all started in 1971 when a 20-foot wall space was painted by neighborhood children. Look for images of fetuses, flowers and solidarity. At #16 there are repeated spraypainted stencil images of protesters with their fists and voices raised in anger. Mission District mural tours are offered by **Precita Eyes Mural Arts Center** (2981 24th St., 285-2287). They also sell mural image postcards and art supplies, and offer art classes for the community.

66 Balmy Gallery (66 Balmy Alley, 648-1760) Search for the door hidden in the murals and enter this scrubbed garage space. See work by the next Jean Michel Basquiat. The adjoining backyard is used for their crowded openings. There are plans to open a second location in the Castro.

The Warehouse (3075 21st St., 235-9552) Nightly happenings at this community center range from open studio paintings to AA meetings. Last summer the Boon Project staged "the TV Show." My favorite installation was a little room, walls covered with typically offensive ads from women's magazines, a gold velour armchair in front of a TV. Infomercial clips flashed on the screen with new voiceovers like "Your toilet smells like someone just shit in it."

SOMA

Stop in front of **1286 Folsom** and pay your respects to the building that once housed **Artspace**, site of many fine shows in the '80s. Jenny Holzer, General Idea, a noisy one by Mark Pauline. Back then I was young and free and had time to see them all, sigh.

New Langton Arts (1246 Folsom St., 626-5416) See and hear the latest new projects in literature, music, net art, performance, video, and visual art. The entry's table offers announcements about other shows around town. Climb the steep, steep stairs to the 2nd story gallery. Be prepared for a group show of edgy work that deals with difficult human issues in a remote, impersonal way. There's an easy access bathroom up here, too. Shows are bimonthly, as they share the space with Cameraworks. See below

Cameraworks Gallery and Bookstore (1246 Folsom, 863-1001) The weirdest images I have ever seen were at Cameraworks at its previous location: huge photos of luridly colored assholes - not jerky people but the real puckered things! Of course they also show more conventional portraiture of prison inmates and other emotional beings as well. Buy a box of postcards by Nan Goldin or Duane Michals.

The Luggage Store (1007 Market, 255-5971) They don't sell luggage but they do provide a cultural oasis in the midst of SF's skid row. There was an intersection of both worlds when an artist removed the large front window to create an installation that pigeons entered and activated. There's a small mural by Margaret Kilgallen (rest in peace) on their metal security gate. They also sponsor the **In the Street Festival** held every autumn, call for info.

111 Minna Gallery (111 Minna St., 974-1719) 111 Minna is never open during its posted business hours but everyone loves it anyway. Openings here are fun, very social, and see-and-be-scene. The Juxtapoz-style art can be okay, too.

CIVIC CENTER / HAYES STREET

San Francisco Arts Commission Gallery (401 Van Ness Ave., 554-6080) Multicultural artists are grouped around themes like Film (as both a medium and a subject) or Immigration. They also program exhibitions in City Hall (across the street) and site specific installations at 155 Grove Street (around the corner)

364 Hayes Street (364 Hayes St., 431-0364) When I entered this pristine space I felt like Holly Golightly in Tiffany's, nothing terrible could ever happen to a girl in here. Sweet memories of youth were arranged lovingly on the walls; plastic leaves, hair pins, soap holders molded from pink plastic. Myriad insignificant objects added up to something much bigger and cleaner than real life.

Velvet da Vinci (508 Hayes St., 626-7478) Fabulous jewelry and metal arts are sold and displayed here. Everything is lovely in a unique way. A bracelet made from bicycle reflectors hinged together with silver. A copper wire insect. A rope chain necklace with a tiny silver tree trunk pendant. Bring your Sugar Daddy or Momma and whine for a treat.

Non-art FYI: Eat at **Frjtz** (579 Hayes, 864-7654) for the best french fries on the planet. **Manifesto** (514 Octavia, 431-4778) has great retro-inspired clothes by a local design team.

DOWNTOWN

49 Geary This building is packed with galleries. The art is expensive so tuck in your shirt. Here are the top three: **Catharine Clark** (399-1439) Risk-taking shows have featured videos starring the artist wearing spandex and false eyelashes, paintings in futuristic taffy colors and pornographic cartoons. **Cheryl Haines** (397-8114) She represents Andy Goldsworthy (in case you're in love with him after seeing that film *Rivers and Tides*). **Fraenkel** (981-2661) Really nice photos from yesterday (WeeGee, Berenice Abbot) and today (Nan Goldin and Richard Avedon).

Gallery Paule Anglim (14 Geary, 433-2710) shows established Bay Area greats like Jay Defeo and Bruce Conner and younger stars like Rigo 2002 and Barry McGee. She even let McGee (aka Twist) break a hole in the sheetrock for his last show. There's a broom hanging near the entrance. I've always wondered, is it art?

FYI: Art Gallery Openings are a good source of FREE food, drink, and sometimes even interesting art. Traditionally, the first Thursday of every month is when many receptions happen. 49 Geary Street is home to a bunch of galleries, and 250 Sutter has three. Check listings in the *Bay Guardian*, or the Sunday *Chronicle*'s Pink Section for more.

THE MUSIC SCENE
BY BETH LISICK

Now that the dotcom fairydust has settled and many of us have begun paying our rent by participating in focus groups culled from **Craig's List** (www.craigslist.com), the San Francisco music scene would like to thank you for standing by during the widespread reports of its demise.

Admittedly, one can still raise the roof with alarmingly regularity enjoying those off the hook cover bands we've been known for in the national press. The city is awash with smart musicians who make extra scratch "moonlighting" in any number of tribute bands. Whether it's Neil Diamond, Burt Bacharach, Charles Mingus or Miles Davis, you can get your nostalgia on just about any night of the week. Check out the calendars for **Bruno's** (2389 Mission at 20th St., 648-7701), **Bimbo's** (1025 Columbus at Broadway, 474-0365) or **The Elbo Room** (647 Valencia at 18th St., 552-

7788) if this is what you're after.

Anyone jonesing to relive the city's former trash rock heyday should look no further than the sweaty upstairs enclave of **Kimo's** (1351 Polk at Pine St., 885-4535) or Oakland's debauched rock den **The Stork Club**. Longtime drag bar Kimo's simply boarded up the windows to prevent neighbor complaints and then launched their full scale assault on decibel police and tastemakers citywide. Though the type of music always depends on what night of week you're visiting, these two clubs have cheap cover charges, tiny stages, bad sightlines, and feature some of the best noisy rock bands around. Metallica recently played a secret show at Kimo's under an assumed name. Touring bands, mostly from LA or the Pacific Northwest, show up often on the club's six-night-a-week schedule.

Nearby, the **Hemlock Tavern** (131 Polk at Post, 923-0923) is the latest cool addition to the local scene where indie-rock bands play 7 nights a week.

Over in the Mission, the recently relaunched **Bruno's** (2389 Mission at 20th St., 648-7701) is fast becoming the city's answer to NYC's Knitting Factory, complete with padded walls and a sidewalk ticket booth. Featuring national acts like trumpeter Dave Douglas, keyboardist Wayne Horvitz and saxophonist Odean Pope, the club also embraces inventive local talents like Beth Custer, Etienne de Rocher and goes SRO for weekend dates with Ledisi and Zoe Ellis. And check into Berkeley's Acme Observatory series at **Tuva** for some of these same acts (and also folks who are way more out.) Tickets are super affordable, but they don't serve fancy cocktails either. BYOB.

When the **Justice League** (628 Divisadero at Hayes, 440-0409) seized a golden opportunity to take an old nightclub and completely reinvent it, they put an ear to the street and have left it there ever since. You can get hip hop, soul, reggae, jazz and all which crosses in between. Even Japanese collage king Cornelius and Kathleen Hannah's Le Tigre stop in. The bookers know what's happening and aren't afraid to take risks.

What would Sunday nights be without the **Make-Out Room** (3225 2nd St. at Mission, 647-2888)? Rely on owner Martin Rapalski's adventures in booking to consistently turn up something new. Lo-fi, klezmer, country, pop and big can-shaking parties with New Orleans-style brass band Brass Monkey. And if you don't like the music, you can't deny that fact that every band on earth looks perfect against the backdrop of those stately red curtains.

Packing them in every other Monday evening at the **Cafe du Nord** (2170 Market, 861-5016) is Eric Shea and Molly Tuttle's Hoot Night. Showcasing an eclectic mix of the Bay Area's best singer-songwriters like Virgil Shaw, Todd Costanza and Carrie Bradley, you'll wish you smuggled in your mini disc recorder.

It's painful how incomplete this list is. (Especially because I'm keeping it strictly legal.) Over the past few years, there has been a resurgence of groups booking private venues like the **Verdi Club** (2424 Mariposa, 861-9199) the **Swedish American Hall** (2174 Market at Church, 431-7578) or bars like Haight St.'s **Peacock Lounge** (552 Haight, 621-9850) to create their own scenes or clubs. And check out what any neighborhood bar is up to during off nights. Some of the most memorable shows I've seen were planned a couple days ahead of time and "publicized" word of mouth. Displacement, astro rents, coppers and pesky neighbors be damned. There may be a lot to complain about in the "new" San Francisco, but we're still here and the soundtrack is good.

MUSIC SCENE

Where and how to find music you might appreciate:

The Weekly Papers: Indispensable for getting the lowdown on what's happening in a given week. Familiarize yourself with the names of the music writers and figure out whose opinion you trust. If you see an ad that says a band features "former members of" some famous band you like, be warned that the former member could be the band's bass player in their first lineup before they ever made a record. If the bands listed in a club's advertisement are different than the ones in the paper's "music listings" section, trust the ad. The club pays for the ad, while the listings are a free service.

College Radio – Great music and ticket giveaways from some of the best college radio stations in the country.

KUSF 90.3 – University of San Francisco
KALX 90.7 – UC Berkeley
KFJC 89.7 – Foothill Junior College
KZSU 90.1 – Stanford University
KSJS 90.5 – San Jose State University

SF Station (www.sfstation.com) - The music section on this site is really impressive. Their editorial staff recommends shows on a daily basis and the venue section is extremely detailed and up-to-date.

Bay Improviser (www.bayimproviser.com) - Call it free jazz, improv, new music or experimental, the Bay Area has one of the hottest scenes for "outside" music around. Must be something in the air that attracts people who play their guitars with forks, buzz cymbals with vibrators and perform duets with hives of honeybees.

SF Indie List (sf_indie-subscribe@yahoogroups.com) - A listerv chock full of local musicians and fans dishing about music, gossiping about each other and promoting their records and upcoming shows. You have to register first and then you can receive an email digest or read the posts on the website. It's informative, fun and sometimes a bit catty. This is also a great place to find out about cheap or free warehouse parties with live music.

Clubs • Lots of clubs have music for little or no door charge, call ahead to find out how much and who's playing. Also, always bring your I.D. to prove you're over 21 (even if you're 30). This is by no means a complete list of venues, just some of 'em.

Blues

The Blue Lamp is a funky little dive featuring blues and more. (561 Geary at Jones, 885-1464).

The Boom-Boom Room (1601 Fillmore and Geary, 673-8000) used to owned by legendary bluesman John Lee Hooker and is still going strong.

Rock

Bottom of the Hill hosts local and indie touring rock bands. (1233 17th St. at Missouri, 626-4455)

The Make-Out Room hosts an eclectic roster of local indie bands, Sundays and Mondays. (3225 22nd St. at Mission, 647-2888)

The Hemlock Tavern (1131 Polk at Post, 923-0923) has a front bar and cozy back room, smoking lounge, and indie rock music 7 nights a week.

DNA is a fun place to go dancing, and is open after-hours, though no alcohol after 2 a.m. (375 11th St. at Folsom,

626-1409)

The Fillmore is one of the most renown concert venues in the U.S. and is still an amazing place to see bands. Nationally-known bands usually. (1805 Geary at Fillmore, 346-6000, www.thefillmore.com)

Great American Music Hall, with its majorly stylin' interior, is one of the all-time great places to see live music. (859 O'Farrell at Polk, 885-0750)

Hotel Utah is a low-key bar with original music by local bands (500 4th St. at Bryant, 546-6300)

Slim's is a rather nondescript room where some really great bands play. Bands playing here today will often be playing a bigger venue next time around. Mostly national, some local. (333 11th St. at Folsom, 255-0333)

Jazz

Elbo Room (647 Valencia at 18th St., 552-7788) has lots of cool jazz upstairs and a decent bar downstairs.

Cavernous DJ Dance Clubs

Ten15 changes every night of the week, house, funk, '70s, whatever. (1015 Folsom at 6th St., 431-1200, www.1015.com)

Townsend's closed for now, but the home of Pleasuredome and Club Universe may open again soon. (177 Townsend at 3rd St., 289-2008)

Raves

Most of the rave scene has moved to the clubs just mentioned, but for time and place details, pick up a handful of colorful invites at **ESDI Records** (1322 Haight near Masonic, 252-1440).

RECORD STORES
BY DENISE SULLIVAN

Used to be traveling collectors and Bay Area record hounds called Berkeley Mecca but not so anymore. The City is the place to shop for new, used and vintage longplayers these days and that's because of **Amoeba Music** (1855 Haight at Stanyan, 831-1200) undisputedly, the hub of all buying, selling and trading activity. Move east on Haight to its lower, less-overrun-by-skaters-and-tourists blocks and you'll find five more vinyl & CD emporia: **Recycled Records** (1377 Haight at Masonic, 626-0563) has a "secret" cellar which has played host to a body-guarded Michael Jackson, among other seekers of all things vinyl and delicious. Groove Merchant caters to the turntablist while **Jack's Record Cellar** (254 Scott at Page, 431-3047) swings toward blues, rare groove and 78 & 45 rpm collectors; **Open Mind** (342 Divisadero at Haight, 621-2244) is where trainspotting collectors and closet jam-band fans converge. Finally, cut through Duboce Park back to Market Street and do a driveby on three more shops on the record trading route: **Streetlight** (2350 Market at Castro, 282-8000) **Medium Rare** (2310 Market at Castro, 255-7273) and **Grooves Inspiralled Vinyl** (1797 Market at Octavia, 436-9933). There's also a **Tower** in the mix (Market at Noe, 621-0588). And if you can bear stretching your legs for a couple more minutes (or battling parking again), travel the 10 extra blocks toward **Aquarius** (1055 Valencia at Hill, 647-2272) for all things San Franciscan and Indie-rock.

If you still insist on crossing the bridge in the name of your vinyl fetish, a similar guerilla plan can be executed within a couple of hours: Start at Telegraph Avenue where Amoeba's original location meets East Bay institution Rasputin's. What you don't find in the used bins there, you'll find at indie and British import and rarity specialists Mod Lang (yes, named for the Big Star song). And if you're still in need of some country blues or old jazz 78s, Down Home music is on your way back to the grid-locked, westerly I-80. Take a tip and ride the BART to Berkeley. Most of the stores sell record carry-bags customized with their own logos—it's the long-distance record-shopper's handy and environment-friendly alternative to all those bags you'd otherwise be carrying home filled with precious CD and vinyl booty.

The Castro

Grooves Inspiralled Vinyl (1797 Market at Octavia, 436-9933) Grooves features tons of what old wavers call vinyl and what even older wavers call wax. In other words, no digital silver discs are sold at Grooves Vinyl Attractions. But don't go thinking you're gonna find the best in audiophile virgin vinyl either: Spacerockers looking for "God Speed You Black Emperor!" or DJs in search of the latest beat break discs need not apply. If you're looking for trendy stuff to drop into the mix, forget that too—it all will have been snagged. So what in the name of Samhain do they carry? Well for one, this is the specialty stop for striptease and gearhead music enthusiasts—the emphasis being on vintage titles. Tons of rare, mint, beat-up, stinky, perfect old records from blues and bebop, folk and funk to mo' slabs o' black wax representing just about every country and small republic of the world are in mucho stocko. Forget trendy and become a trendsetter on the wheels of steel: Drop an old Scottish bagpipe record or something spoken by Vincent Price into the mix; throw on a crackly Neil Young rarity or a classic metal LP (hello that copy of Master of Puppets you put off buying all these years) and drive your friends crazy! There are literally tons of records for under $5 from which to choose—ones that you didn't even know you wanted like Folk Songs of India or the LP that houses that top 40 nugget "Vehicle" by Ides of March. Plus, there's plenty more '90s and '70s rock at good prices—jazz too. But the real action is in the $1 bin where along with the usual castoffs (Dan Fogelberg) you'll find the odd must-add-to-the-collection-title (John Prine's "Bruised Orange," with it's persimmon-bright inside cover, in mint condition!). Okay, so it's a little musty in the joint (you might see the co-owner sportin' protective gloves and face mask from time to time)—but then no one said that vinyl collecting would be easy at the dawn of the 21st Century.

Also in the 'hood

Record Finder (258 Noe at Market, 431-4443) New release titles at used prices, rarities at rarity prices, buy/sell/trade.

Medium Rare (2310 Market at Sanchez, 255-7273) From Ethel Mermen to Esquivel plus theremin, exotica and electica.

Streetlight Records (2350 Market at Noe, 278-9550) New and used, buy/sell/trade; a handy, all-purpose independent record store.

Tower Records (Market at Noe, 621-0588) A Tower is a Tower, but always reliable for those major label "nice price" $7.98 catalog titles.

The Haight

Amoeba Music (1855 Haight at Stanyan, 831-1200)

Touted as "the world's largest record store," Amoeba (with locations in Berkeley and Los Angeles) is a mind-boggling airplane hangar of a retail outlet (over 1,000,000 discs) that's even equipped with a stage and two turntables and a microphone for in-store appearances (they've all played here, from Joe Strummer and Elliott Smith to the Invisbl Skratch Picklz). Every kind of music is available under one high ceiling from which very clear section signs hang, pointing you toward "Reggae" and "Used Reggae" for example (where you'll find no lie, the biggest Bob Marley selection outside of Kingston). The world music section is mighty impressive—from Sufi dance music to Ali Farka Toure—and there's even a separate, subdued annex for jazz and classical titles just in case you needed a fresh-press of Coltrane's "A Love Supreme." But what we all go there for are the bargains. The main attraction are the "used" CDs, never-before-played promotional titles that get dropped there by the box load, with the discount getting passed on to you, the ever-lovin' consumer. So whether you're jonesin' for Rod Stewart croonin' "Maggie May" or Alice Cooper screechin' "school's out... fore-ever!" you want it, they got it in the $1 bin alongside some classic new wave titles by the Motels and the Cars. A word of warning: you'll literally be on your hands and knees fetching that perfect vinyl catch.

Also in the 'hood

Recycled Records (1377 Haight at Masonic, 626-4075) A cellar full of records and Lord knows what else housed at the perfect gateway to the Haight-Ashbury location. The original SF buy/sell/trade store, new is not really a concept here.

Groove Merchant (687 Haight at Pierce, 252-5766) With its reputation for rare soul and funk grooves (the Beastie Boys name-checked them in a song), this is the one-stop shop for turntablists and turntable music enthusiasts who like to play front-room DJ.

Open Mind Music (342 Divisadero at Page, 621-2244) Buy/sell/trade, new and used, specializing in good taste & rarities, "from Abba to Zappa" in the stacks, to Crazy Horse bassist Billy Talbot seen shopping the racks.

Jack's Record Cellar (254 Scott at Page, 431-3047) In business since 1951 Jack's serves up R&B, jazz 45s and 78s by the knowledgeable and uniquely overqualified staff (former Flamin' Groovie and perennial rocker Roy Loney shines up discs and your collection, from his post behind-the-counter).

Off-the-beaten-track

Aquarius Records (1055 Valencia at Hill, 647-2272) Aquarius was among the first to carry punk rock 45s, back in the day. Today they specialize in local and international indie-rock, from Blackalicious and Death Cab for Cutie to Os Mutantes. Yum-yum.

Berkeley/East Bay

Mod Lang (2136 University at Shattuck, 510-486-1880) Specializing in all things indie and British, new and used, Mod Lang is also the place to haunt for rare psychedelic, folk and progressive rock needs, from reissues to rarities. An incredible back stock of punk and new wave awaits the collector who dares to ask for it.

Rasputin Music (2401 Telegraph at Channing, 800-350-8700) It takes some pickin' and your feet and hands may take a lickin' but this classic, East Bay new and used record warehouse will almost always hold a treasure for those willing to pan for gold amidst the gravel.

Amoeba Music (2455 Telegraph at Dwight, 510-549-1125) Again, worth a trip if you're in the neighborhood but not a destination record store in itself. Amoeba has one trump card though: They'll pay top prices for all the used junk you can drag out of your basement (and everyone else's you know).

Down Home Music (10341 San Pablo, El Cerrito; 510-525-2129) Don't let its outside the people's republic of Berkeley city limits dissuade you: Down Home is worth the trundle for the new and used folk, blues and folk-blues, among other traditional music. Know all those creaky 78 tunes on the Ghostworld and Crumb soundtracks? You can bet your last crawdad they were picked up here.

UNDERGROUND MUSICIANS' GUIDE
BY DENISE SULLIVAN

Ever since the '60s, musicians (and other artists) have run away to San Francisco for the artist-friendly climate, diverse scene and tolerance. Of course the '90s had a lot musicians heading for the hills when the dot-conomy forced unprecedented high rents and evictions; studio, practice and club spaces closed in record numbers. So what's a resourceful SF musician to do? Dig deeper, and find the sweet deals. And whether you're an acoustic guitar slinger, a turntablist or looking to join a queer punk band, there are rooms in which to live, work and play in town. By no means a definitive list, these free and low-cost services for musicians will take you from getting started to releasing your own CD, all on a meager musician's wage.

THE WANT ADS

Traditionally, the help wanted ads in the free weeklies and music papers were the way to find that Bass Player Wanted or to list yourself, as in Singer Looking For a Band. With the advent of online communities, the two places you'll want to look first (say, for that fiddle player with a passion for goth) are craigslist.org and sfmusician.com Both feature listings for players, gear, lessons, CD manufacturing and miscellaneous services like publicists and photographers for hire. There is no charge to browse the listings and posting is free.

www.craigslist.org

www.sfmusician.com

PRACTICE SPACE

The Point (an artist's community at the city's defunct port site) at Hunter's Point Shipyard, remains home to a number of studio spaces—but the only way to find a place there is to look for "For Rent" signs or to hang one of your own in the neighborhood (the official waiting list for The Point is about two years long). The classifieds at craigslist.org and sfmusician.com both carry a bunch of listings for bands looking to share spaces and there are commercial spaces that advertise deals there too. For example, Sound Design Studios offers a $10 per hour rate (not bad if you only practice a couple of hours a week and don't need storage). If that fails, you could do like a number of resourceful players have been known to do: rent yourself a self-storage space and rock out there.

The Point, Hunter's Point Shipyard (Innes at Donahue, 822-9675)

Sound Design Studios (555 Fulton, Suite 201-B, 252-7200)

INSTRUMENTS/ACCESSORIES

Subway Guitars (1800 Cedar, Berkeley; 510-841-4106) legendary proprietor, Fatdog, prides himself on hooking up each and every one of his customers with the perfect guitar—at a price that's easy on the wallet. He'll make you a custom guitar out of new/old parts and only charge one-half to one-third of what you'd normally expect to pay; he carries discontinued lines like Coral, Vox, Kay and Danelectro and brand new factory models too. Trade-ins are "seriously considered." Sales, repairs, parts and accessories—all are on offer at rock bottom prices. And Subway isn't just about guitars—there are basses, amps, drums and other stringed instruments too. Fatdog and Subway have offered a way of life for 30 years: Music for the people, by the people, at only 25% above wholesale.

INSTRUCTION

Bay Area musicians of every level and style, from surf, rockabilly and punk to country, jazz and blues, know that the **Professor Sludge Guitar Academy** (Professor Sludge Guitar Academy, www.professorsludge.com, 239-5390) is the place to go when they want to beef up their skills. For 10 years, Bay Area musician Eric Lenchner, a.k.a. Sludge, has been teaching professionals the basics—like how to play and sing at the same time(!). He also teaches music theory, songwriting technique, transcribing and how to teach. He'll also help to take you from baby student to proficient player (he's taught children as young as 4). Prices vary for the half hour and hour long private sessions—and people have been known to bring a friend along to cut costs. Call Sludge for more concrete details.

ANALOG RECORDING STUDIOS

For just $35 an hour (not including engineer) do-it-yourself musicians (from locals Chuck Prophet and the Residents to out-of-towner Frank Black) take care of their tracking needs at **The Studio That Time Forgot** (253 Capp at 17th St., 255-7020), a no-frills place with high quality equipment for analog recording. Owner and engineer Kevin

Ink presides over the two-inch 24-track machine and Neve console. With a large room for tracking drums, it's a musician-friendly place, meaning he's got a mind-boggling assortment of vintage mics and other equipment laying around the freewheelin' warehouse—but no lounge area or pinball machines, dig? John Vanderslice's Tiny Telephone (www.tinytelephone.com, 642-1970) studio is indie-rock central and gets booked way in advance by bands like Mates of State and Beulah. The day rate is $550, including an engineer with access to the half-inch mix-down deck, a tuned control room, good monitors, automated faders, the works— including a lounge! Vanderslice's place also boasts the desirable mid-'70s Neve console and the credo, No Pro Tools. Book 'em, Dano.

CD MASTERING, DUPLICATION AND MANUFACTURING

Need 25 CDRs for your friends, 2500 CDs to sell at gigs or 25,000 to as part of your band's plan for world domination? Then head to **Olde West** ((3130 20th St. at Harrison, 647-7100), the number one supplier of all things related to CD manufacturing 'round these parts, including mastering facilities. All you need to do is show up with music and artwork and they'll take care of the rest (though they stress that distribution is up to you!). For more specifics on quantities, pricing and discounts, Wes or Brian will explain the details over the phone.

OPEN MIC NIGHTS

The open mic night might sound like an old wave way to break into the business but Mondays at **Hotel Utah** (500 4th St. at Bryant, 546-6300) are as good a time as any to dip your toe into the live, local scene. As one of San Francisco's oldest watering holes, this funky, low-ceilinged Barbary Coast-style bar is a landmark on the live performance and bar scene. SF bands like American Music Club and Red House Painters (both of whom played their earliest gigs there) are alumnus of the scene where every Monday newcomers line-up for the chance to play a short set in front of a genuinely decent crowd of fellow musicians and long-time super-fans of local music. From shy, beginning singer-songwriters and familiar faces testing out new material to alterna-bands bashing it up, the Utah's open mic is a good hang—a place to be among your people, as well as to be seen, get heard and have a good time—and best of all, it's free for performers.

In Berkeley, the **Freight & Salvage** (1111 Addison at San Pablo, Berkeley; 510-548-1761) coffeehouse, a folk music institution, hosts the Bay Area's longest running open stage (the club opened in '68). Traditional, regional and ethnic music are the Freight's stock-in-trade so electronica fanatics, turntablists and rockers need not apply (though that's not to say that adventurous music is discouraged). Call the club because the nights of the week vary from month to month; music always starts at 8 at the Freight.

EAR CARE

A musician's number one on-the-job hazard is hearing loss. That's why in 1988, punk rocker Kathy Peck (from the all-girl SF band, the Contractions) had the bright idea to start **H.E.A.R.** (Hearing Education and Awareness for Rockers) (PO Box 460847, 409-3277, www.hearnet.com), dedicated to the prevention of hearing loss and tinnitus among musicians, fans and industry professionals. Take advantage of services like fittings for earplugs and hearing devices, and lessons on hearing prevention. Open in the evenings by appointment (send them an email), hearing tests are offered on a sliding scale or donation basis.

READING FRENZY
BY JON LONGHI

If all the ink in the world were to suddenly vanish, publishers in San Francisco would print things in their own blood. This same kind of barnacle tough determination extends to the fog city's underground bookstores. Relentlessly alternative, dismissing the New York Times Best Seller List and Publisher's Weekly Top 10 as mere hallucinations of a brain-dead society, most local book and magazine shops instead surf the fringes, always looking for new mind candy to please the diverse plethora of subcultures making up this city's social body. From highbrow academic theory to the lowest, most filthy pornography, they offer it all. Most retailers are also supportive of the local publishing community to a degree that few other stores around the country are. Many even go so far as to stock handmade editions and zines. For out-of-towner and resident alike, there is the special treat of obtaining raw literary and artistic gems found no place else.

The feverish pitch of creative activity in the Bay Area often leads one to believe it is some kind of hallucinogenic art colony. On a percentage basis, San Francisco and its environs probably crank out more art than any other city on the planet. This imagination extends to the merchandisers themselves. Stores in this town are downright gaudy with personality. Many places are quasi-entities combining things like bone collections, tattooists, hair salons, books, tapes, fortune-telling, and periodicals, all in one establishment. Oh yes, coffee is also usually involved. For a lover of books, many a listless afternoon can be euphorically killed poking through arcane and hypnotic collections.

I can think of no better place to start than **City Lights Bookstore** (261 Columbus at Broadway, 362-8193, www.citylights.com). Nestled in the bosom of North Beach, less than a shotglass throw from some of the most notorious beatnik dives, City Lights functions as both museum and breeding ground. Almost every literary classic of the human language is available. Literature from around the world and around the block share shelf space in a kind of modern day Library of Alexandria which can devour weeks of time just in the act of browsing. The consignment area in the back has one of the best selections of small press/chapbook/zine/ handmade object/literary journal publications available anywhere. The work in these things is uneven, but the pearls to be found in their pages harbor the real future of literature. And if it's the past you prefer, City Lights provides a choice which stretches back before Beowulf, earlier than Ovid, to Homer and beyond. Philosophy, art, history, and fiction, it's all there. An entire room upstairs is devoted to poetry, offering one of the most comprehensive assortments in the U.S. All conveniently located across the street from Spec's and next door to Vesuvio's, two bars you can drink at and have an experience worthy of writing a poem about, or at least an adventure novel. I don't really have a religion, so City Lights is the closest thing I have to a church in this town. Ain't it time you did a little work on your soul?

Now let's shift channels quickly across town to the Haight, San Francisco's boho paradise of inebriation, piercing, tattoos, and general alternative brouhaha. Without a doubt, the best magazine store in this neighborhood and possibly the best in the city is **Naked Eye** (533 Haight at Fillmore; 864-2985). Stocking this store has been a labor of love, and it carries everything from Time and Playboy to slick top-of-the-line fetish journals and magazines devoted to Asian Trash Cinema. A variety of locally and nationally produced zines share space with the rest. And if movies are your cup of tea, Naked Eye has a videotape/DVD selection that will make even the most jaded alternative hipper-than-thou bend over and hurl with delight. Midnight movies, splatter flicks, art loops, rockumentaries, foreign films, documentaries, Japanese monster movies, enough variety to pick every tooth in a culture vulture's beak. Over five thousands titles. Five thousand! Do you know how many hours that is? And that's only if you can get past the magazines without spending every penny and wearing out your last synapse. There are books and movies at this store that I've never seen anyplace else. There's something here to document even the most obscure fringe.

Slide on up the hill to where Divisadero severs Haight Street and a short distance to your right is **Comix Experience** (305 Divisadero at Oak; 863-9258), a world class comic book shop. Yeah, I know it's a comic store and not a book store, but comics are literature, so get used to it, okay? A healthy showing of undergrounds soak up shelf space and the miasmal aura of Todd McFarlane is remarkably dim.

The people who work there are mellow and extremely intelligent. If you're looking for a title, ask them, they'd probably be familiar with it. A shimmering cornucopia of psychedelic colors and pictorial story lines make up the Comix Experience, there's more there than you could ever put on your tongue.

Up the hill, next to a shady courtyard on Haight Street, sits **Bound Together** (1369 Haight at Masonic; 431-8355), the creme de la creme of anarchist bookstores. The outer walls of the collective display scrawled political slogans and a glowing mural. Inside is an anarchist's candy shop. For the armchair intellectual there are the collected works of great reformers and political thinkers throughout history, while the street fighter can peruse manuals on how to build bombs and Molotov cocktails. Most of the Bound Together staff have a greater knowledge of politics, both contemporary and historical, than one could ever squeeze out of a poli-sci prof on any campus, and best of all, you won't have to listen to any intellectual ass-kissing of the latest French darling of academia. Beliefs at this store are not molded by tenure, but they stock all the French philosophers anyway. Almost no idea is excluded from this place, no matter how controversial or unpopular. In fact there are so many voices available at Bound Together that even when the store is empty it seems deafening. On their shelves are voices you have been listening for all your life, voices that will change your life, voices that you agree with, disagree with; there will even be voices that annoy and outrage you. That's the point. Bound Together is one of the few bookstores in the country that is immune to the censor's amputation. As a result, the place is many limbed like Shiva, a deafening palette of clashing ideas, so many books, so many voices, a model of pure anarchy made from pictures and printed words, where the only thing that binds it all together is the collective's devotion to complete freedom and access to any and all information.

Now for information of a lighter-headed nature one need only walk across the street to **Pipe Dreams** (1376 Haight at Central; 431-3553). Pipe Dreams stocks some of the finest tobacco accessories and waterpipes west of Amsterdam. They also carry books. Besides tomes bursting with information for recreational growers, one can peruse rock fanzines, and a mutant variety of underground publications. There's always something there guaranteed to light up every taste.

A stone's throw away dwells **Anubis Warpus** (1525 Haight at Ashbury; 431-2218). It's one of a growing breed of places where you can buy a book about tattoos, bring it to the back of the store, and have their resident skin artist put your favorite design directly onto your flesh. Or if you just want to get a couple holes poked in your Johnson, they have facilities for that too. One can see a rainbow there just in the hair dyes that adorn the customers' heads. The fine selection of magazines and books take up an entire wall and radiate a fashionably bad attitude. Two tall bookcases are given over to erotic publications and the selection covers the distance from slick high end latex fashion catalogues down to xerox zines singing the praises of fat dykes and transsexuals. Comics, rock books, hip lit titles, and tomes of post modern theory flesh out this eclectic mix. They also sell clothes and t-shirts.

Just a short hop down the street is **Booksmith** (1644 Haight at Clayton; 863-8688). Booksmith has all the front list selection that a mainstream Barnes & Noble or Borders has, only the roots of their selection sink much deeper into the underground. Numerous small press offerings share shelf space with the classics. From street level literature to punk rock rants, these edges are where all the fun is. Say you want to buy a copy of Betty Page in Bondage trading cards or Peter Plate's latest novel, Booksmith has got them. They even branch out into fetish titles and deviant philosophy. The art department boasts one of the best selections of full-color hardcovers to be found in the city, while the magazine rack provides hours of fun.

That kind of finishes the Haight Street ramble, but if we move over to the Richmond, one finds another of San Francisco's premier book dens. **Green Apple Books** (506 Clement at 6th Avenue; 387-2272) has the musty dusty feel of the best old town libraries. There is a rustic and romantic atmosphere to the narrow alleys which wind between shelves which often reach up to the ceilings. There's something mysterious and magical about the character of the building itself, like it was just dropped here by a tornado from Kansas or something. Inside, it's all a crazed mix of the old and new. Out of print, used, and rare tomes are mixed in with the newest stuff. The front of the store assaults you with the hot off the press best sellers, but for my money the best finds are to be mined from the deeper aisles which wind like caves through two stories of rooms. Great old sci-fi, and detective noir pulps can be scored there. The art books section is one of the best, lots of discounted hardcovers and crisp color reproductions. They stock a great graphic novel section, and the store has a long history of being supportive of underground, small press, and local publishers. Don't go there if you're in a hurry. It's the kind of place you want to poke around in for ages.

Now let's shift gears rapidly over to the Mission District. **Modern Times** (888 Valencia at 20th St.; 282-9246), is one of those few places that take the idea of "diversity" seriously. Though they tend to steer towards the highbrow and intellectual, their selection is a monument to multiculturalism. So many races and civilizations seem to glow on its shelves. They have a rich philosophy section which seamlessly documents the span from ancient to contemporary. The great works of Eastern and Western civilization can be found there, as well as samplings from all other points of the compass. It's a selection that reminds one of the inherent dignity of the human condition. That's not to say that they're fuddy-duddy. If you need a quick manual on S/M or the latest stroke book from Cleis Press, they'll probably have them too. The gay and lesbian section is sumptuous, the sci-fi and horror section divine. They even have a reading space in the back which frequently hosts some of the literary luminaries of our time. It's one of the few book peddlers out there where there truly is something for everyone.

Down the block, **Borderlands** (866 Valencia, 558-8978) has incredible ambience: the bookshelves and interior exude a warm personality that makes you want to hang out and browse for hours. It's arguably one of the best science fiction bookstores in the country containing a spectrum of speculative fiction from early classics by Lovecraft, Blackwood, and Wells to the latest cyberpunk. Out-of-print and rare titles share shelf space with zines and handmade chapbooks, and the helpful, knowledgeable staff is enthusiastic about their books, too.

Two of the best used bookstores in the city are **Dog Eared Books** (900 Valencia St.; 282-1901) and their sister store **Phoenix Books** (3850 24ᵗʰ St.; 821-3477). If you're the type who's life has recently been consumed by the search for a certain out of print book, then Dog Eared or Phoenix may have your Holy Grail. The shelves at both stores are fat with a tremendous and eclectic variety of art and literary books. And they don't just do used; their collections of new titles are also quite plush. Wandering into either of these stores can soak up days of one's existence. The staffs at the stores are witty, intelligent, and helpful. A real cast of characters, the first question on the Phoenix and Dog Eared resume must be are you an interesting person? Owner Kate Rosenberger has always staffed her stores as if she were hiring characters for a magical realism novel instead of booksellers. These people make a great place even better. And if you're ever low on cash they give great cash and trade for your old used books. Taking my old books to Dog Eared has gotten me through many a lean week. What more do you need to know, just go there! Nearby **Adobe Books** (3166 16th St., 864-3936) is another rockin' used bookstore hosting great readings and more.

One of the oldest institutions in the city is Gary Arlington's **San Francisco Comic Book Company** (3335 23rd St., 647-1468). This tiny grotto of comic book treasures was the first store in the US to sell Zap comix and the original psychedelic undergrounds. Drop in and see one of the city's most legendary eccentrics and his little shop of horrors and wonders.

Throughout the Bay Area there's a host of museums and attractions that are truly unique. One of these that no tourist or native should miss is the **Cartoon Art Museum** (814 Mission St. 2nd floor, 227-8666) and **Foto-grafix** (655 Mission St., 495-7242) a terrific art bookstore at the Museum's street-level. It is one of the only museums in the country devoted purely to the study and archiving of sequential art. A single walk through the museum's galleries will provide one with tremendous insight into this misunderstood and maligned art form. The bookstore there is almost a museum in its own right. They have signed editions by famous artists and a selection of graphic novels that spans the spectrum from raw undergrounds to slick mainstream superhero epics. They also sell original artwork by the likes of Mary Wilshire and Charles Schulz. My favorite item is a limited edition signed color lithograph by

Charles Schulz that he did in honor of D-Day. The picture depicts Snoopy meeting General MacArthur.

If you're looking for art books of a more traditional style, just around the corner the bookstore in the **Museum of Modern Art** should satisfy any cultural connoisseur's cravings. It is stocked literally to the ceiling with artist monographs and huge hardcover overviews of every significant art movement in the history of visual representation. Biographies of the likes of Duchamp and Picasso share space with tomes of art theory and criticism. There are enough hardcovers in this one store to cover half the coffee tables in North America. Though the vast majority of their books deal with visual themes, you'll also find a select inventory of other titles there as well. They do a few travel guides and other local interest books and there's a good chance you could even have bought your copy of the *Underground Guide To San Francisco* there.

Another bookstore of note near Union Square is **Kayo Books** (814 Post at Leavenworth, 749-0554), specializing in vintage pulp fiction paperbacks and magazines - you know, the ones with the lascivious covers - and other eclectic publications. Lots of out-of-print classics here, too.

Almost better than any other store in the city, **Bernal Books** (401 Cortland; 550-0293) shows how a well-run bookstore can become the spiritual center of a neighborhood. Owner Rachel Pepper has provided such sensitive outreach with the local community that her bookstore has become a vital part of the neighborhood. She takes requests, provides storytimes for local children, and has a friendly personality that makes you just want to go there to hang out with her as well as browse and buy books. Though small, her store is stocked with elegant literary taste. Each section is well thought out and beautifully organized and displayed, whether it be mainstream fiction, adult novels, or children's books.

A long tenure at Different Light down in the Castro gave Pepper a real talent for bookselling and she turned this to a fine art when she forged out on her own. The friendly neighborhood bookstore is a dying breed in America these days, buried beneath the faceless behemoths of chain stores where the brand of coffee they serve is more important than the number of Nobel Prize winners on the shelves. It is rare to find a place such as Rachel Pepper's which actually has a dialogue with the local community. In such a soulless corporate world, bookstores such as Bernal Books are truly heroic.

One of the premier gay bookstores in the country is **Different Light** (489 Castro St., 431-0891). It has been an institution in the Castro neighborhood for decades. If you're looking for a gay and lesbian title and you don't find it here, you're not going to find it. I work at a book distributor and gay and lesbian titles are one of our strongest lines. I figure I have a fairly good handle on what's out there, but every time I go into Different Light I see books where I haven't even heard of the publisher, much less the title. At times while browsing in Different Light you forget that you are in a bookstore and begin to believe that you are in a shrine to how this community documents itself. Regular readings are held in the back courtyard and some of the performances I have seen there have been legendary for their drama, rage, and power. The bookstore is as integral to the Castro and its history as its neighbor the Castro Theatre.

Books Inc. (2275 Market St., 864-6777) is hipster central. Located across the street from Tower Records and around the corner from the Castro Theatre, it's the perfect place to buy books on an evening out. Located in the middle of a variety of hip restaurants and cafes, Books Inc. is the perfect place to see and be seen. Where else are you going to meet someone who shares a passion for Nietzsche and lesbian bondage? Their shelves are a bright wall of eye candy. The **Books Inc. Outlet** (160 Folsom at Main, 442-4830) has some awesome prices on new and slightly damaged books.

Even by the time you spot its Mats?! painted sign from a half block away, you know that as you creep up on **Al's Comics** (491 Guerrero; 861-1220) you've found someplace special. Comics cover every inch of wall space on the inside from floor to ceiling. Hell, they've probably even got a few pasted on the ceiling, just for that 360 effect. Everything from this week's Marvel and D.C. to lurid pulp mags from the '50s combine to make a collage of action, horror, and a thousand dreams. It's a collector's crack house and one of the few magic places left in this country. A place with personality, good service, and hours of bin digging. Stores that still stock old comics these days are like a breath of fresh air and memories. Where else are you going to find that old comic or monster magazine that totally rocked your world when you were ten years old? Finding one of these old relics from our youth can be more relevant to our understanding ourselves than a whole shoebox full of snapshots. Where else but a place like Al's Comics are you going to be able to reconnect with your past? Where else can you regain all the dreams of childhood?

Two chain stores have earned inclusion in this chapter because they consistently stock a variety of small press, alternative, and underground books and publications. These chain stores that are the exceptions to the usual chain stores are Tower Books and Records and the Virgin Megastore.

If you ask me, the **Virgin Megastore** (2 Stockton St., 397-4525) is a better bookstore than a record store. Its inventory is filled with sumptuous canyons of eye candy and literary treats. On their shelves you can find the latest flavor of the moment hipster author sitting comfortably beside classics like Dostoevski's *Crime and Punishment* and James Joyce's *Ulysses*. Their stock of art books has the same depth and width. The store also carries a great selection of graphic novels. Besides the latest comic anthologies from Vertigo, Dark Horse, Last Gasp and Fantagraphics, you'll also find such rarities as imported French and German graphic novels with art so beautiful it'll make you cry right there in the store. This is the perfect place to waste away an hour browsing.

In **Tower**'s stores in the Bay Area some of the latest mainstream publications from the New York houses sit comfortably next to small press, underground and even zine publications. This ability to cater to all interests and not just those of mainstream suburbia has always been what set Tower apart from the competition. There are Tower stores all over the Bay Area and any one of them is worth checking out, but two with especially great book sections are the ones at Columbus &Bay (885-0500), Market & Noe (621-0588) and the one out in the Stonestown Mall (3205 20th Ave. 2nd Floor; 681-2001). Oh, they also have some pretty cool records there as well. The **Tower Outlet** (660 Third St. near Townsend, 957-9660) has a wacky assortment of CDs at bargain prices, too.

Farley's (1315 18th St. at Texas; 648-1545) is the last stop on our trip and that's a good thing, because their specialty is coffee. Take a walk up Potrero Hill, and kick back in their spacious and well-lit ambiance. Their menu is a java junkie's dream and as you jump start your heart you can sample one of the best stocked magazine racks west of the Pecos. Whether you read *Details*, *Bust*, or *Bitch*, they have it there. The tables around you are often haunted by poets scribbling away in notebooks or artists filling sketchbooks.

Well, that just about does it for me. If you couldn't find

that special book you were looking for by the end of this tour it's not San Francisco's fault. The last copy must have been burned by some Christian fanatic somewhere, or maybe Jesse Helms is hiding it in his bathroom. Long before the end of this tour any sane person able to read past the third grade level would have acquired more books than they could carry. Anyone literate who does the whole tour should be shipping stuff home bulk mail because it's too heavy for the plane. As for me, I'm heading back home to get some reading done.

PLEASURE AND PAIN, POKING AND PAINTING
BY BUCKY SINISTER

Chances are, if you're reading this guide, you're not the average tourist. You're not interested in the "Alcatraz Swim Team" shirts, or having a picture of yourself riding a cable car. No, the best souvenirs are forever: tattoos. If you can't go that far, at least get yourself a nice piercing. Forget about that snowdome of the Golden Gate bridge. It never snows here anyway.

You can spend at least an entire day going and visiting tattooing and piercing places. Take a look at the Yellow Pages and mark up your Muni Map to see what I mean. Every place has its specialties and pros and cons.

TATTOOS
Old School: Two places, near to each other in North Beach, are world famous and should definitely be visited: **Lyle**

Tuttle's (841 Columbus at Lombard, 775-4991) and **Tattoo City** (700 Lombard at Mason, 345-9437). These places and some of the artists have been around since your daddy got your momma's name tattooed on his arm during shore leave. Tattoo City is run by Ed Hardy, who is arguably the most noted historian of the art form.

New School: Of note are two women-owned-and-run shops in the Mission: **Black & Blue Tattoo** (483 14th St. at Guerrero, 626-0770) and **Sacred Rose Tattoo** (491 Guerrero at 17th St., 552-5778).

A FEW TIPS FOR THE ROOKIES

Don't be drunk. There's not a shop in town that will tattoo you drunk. This commonly leads to angry customers coming back the next day saying things like "why in hell do I have a tattoo of Tweety Bird with an erection?" That, and it thins out the blood so you bleed more, and yes, it will hurt anyway.

Watch the location. Keep the work off the hands, fingers, neck, and face. These are hard to conceal, and a "wild child" tattoo on your neck won't look good in job interviews.

Don't feel restricted to the flash on the walls. Ask to see the photo albums of the custom work. This is where you'll see the artist's greatest hits. Don't be shy about asking for something conceptual, like a cobra wearing a fez eating a TV dinner while on his skateboard. Just be warned that included in an artist's hourly fee includes drawing time.

No names. This guarantees you will break up with that special someone. Tattoos are forever. Relationships rarely are.

It's a good time for a cover-up. That tat you got from your best friend in high school done during art class with India Ink and a needle of the Van Halen logo may be costly to remove, but much cheaper to cover up. Every shop has some before and after photos, just ask.

PIERCING

Most places in the country it's now easy to find a place to get one's ear or nose pierced. But if you're looking for something more exotic that will guarantee that the hicks back home will forever ask "didn't that hurt" about, you came to the right place.

There are two main places that pierce: **Cold Steel** (1783 Haight at Cole, 933-7233; also 2377 Market at Castro, 621-7233) and **Body Manipulations** (3234 16th St., 621-0408). Take your time looking around. It's better to go in during a weekday. On the weekend, the shop's fill with gawkers. When there is more time to answer questions (and you should ask), the service is much better.

This may sound obvious, but I should say it anyway. Regarding genital piercings: these can make it difficult to walk around until they start to heal. If you're planning a hike up Mt. Tam the next day, don't do it.

One more tip for both piercing and tattooing. Both of these take time to heal and require careful hygienic maintenance. If you're roadtripping with five other friends in your mom's minivan under the premise that you're looking at colleges and haven't bathed since Omaha, just forget it.

SEX IN THE CITY
BY TARIN TOWERS

San Francisco has been renowned for its sexual appetites since the Gold Rush days, when the Barbary Coast and the Mission District boasted whorehouses and other dens of iniquity that couldn't be equaled elsewhere in the American West. Back then, the exotic thing was opium dens and Chinese women. Now, I have no idea what San Franciscans consider exotic - not even abstinence is without its fetishists.

If you like having sex, you've come to the right place. No matter what your persuasion, there are people in the area who share your proclivities and, more important, who want to get laid. Straight women can complain that there aren't enough straight, single guys around, but folks of all genders and orientations can consider themselves commodities here. It's an easy town to be easy in.

WHAT IS SEX, ANYWAY?

If you're sitting at home wondering whether you're alone in your taste for squash flicks, or if you have a question about staying safe, or even if you're just wondering whether a flashlight could really get stuck up there, ask **San Francisco Sex Information** (989-SFSI, 3 p.m.-9 p.m., www.sfsi.org).

The *SF Bay Guardian* and the *SF Weekly* boast three sex advice columns between them. If you're looking for something less mainstream, though, head to your nearest newsstand (the kind that carries porn), and pick up a copy of the **Spectator** (www.spectator.net). An odd combination of sexual adventure stories, art and entertainment reviews, political essays, scene gossip, and escort and party-line ads, the Spectator makes interesting reading. Note: they offer a great current sex-related events calendar, and listings including sales and rentals.

With internet access, if you want to find something specific to do or learn about, try the **Eros Guide to San Francisco** (www.eros-guide.com), which lists escorts and dominatrix services, among other things. Another decent online listing is the **Pleasure Seeker's Guide to San Francisco** (www.seekerspub.com/sfo/), if you can stand the constant ads for the "Interracial Fuck Orgy."

FLYING SOLO

The mother of all sex shops, **Good Vibrations** (1210 Valencia at 23rd St., 974-8980, www.goodvibes.com) is a woman-owned, queer-friendly, men-too co-op that stocks all the vibrators, butt-plugs, floggers, and weird feathery things you can imagine, and a lot of stuff you probably can't. They also stock quality porn videos and both kinds of sex books: How-to and How-now. If you prefer your sex toys a little more tasteless, try **Big Al's** (556 Broadway at

Columbus, 391-8510), the penis squirt-gun superstore.

The Magazine (920 Larkin at Geary, 441-7737) offers both vintage and contemporary porn (gay, straight, specialty). **Don's of Sixth Street** (111 6th St. at Mission, 543-1656) traffics in used porn, both paper and video, avoiding stuck-together pages. **Leather Tongue** (714 Valencia at 18th St., 552-2900) isn't just for porn, but they have a good adult video section upstairs.

THE LEARNING CHANNEL

Yes, they do offer remedial sex education. **The Learning Annex** (788-5500, www.learningannex.com) offers classes that may or may not be pick-up joints. These are often straight vanilla classes on "How to Make Love to a Man" or "Tantric Lovemaking."

Good Vibrations (see above) actually offers masturbation classes for the orgasm-deprived, as well as workshops on making and using sex toys, having fun safely, and "How to Get What you Want: Sexual Communication and Negotiation," which I think translates as either "How to Get Laid" or "How to Get Your Lover to Do That Thing They Think Is Nasty."

If you want to learn kink from people who know how to hurt you without injuring you, go alone or with your partner to **QSM** (550-7776, www.qualitysm.com). This highly respected school offers books, toys, and a plethora of demonstrations and classes, including "Creative Tit Play," "Embracing the Slave Within," and "Vaginal Fisting: Learn To Do It Right."

YOU WEAR IT WELL

Before you go out on the town, pick up your stomping shoes and your stomping pants. My favorite store for amazing dresses is **Leather Etc.** (1201 Folsom, 864-7558).

Stormy Leather (1158 Howard at 8th St., 626-6783) carries the latest and greatest in leather and latex for women and men of all sizes. BDSM scensters of all genders like shopping for gear at **Mr. S Leather** (310 7th St. at , 863-7764). The ultra-femme might want to order a hand-tailored corset from the geniuses at **Dark Garden** (321 Linden at Octavia, 431-7684, www.darkgarden.com).

Guys who want to try their hand at crossdressing should head for **Piedmont** (1452 Haight at Masonic, 864-8075), highly recommended for friendly service, a great assortment of feather boas, and all the necessary accoutrements for changing one's look genderwise. For classy sleaze apparel, stop by the **Foxy Lady Boutique** (2644 Mission at 23rd St., 285-4980), which features shoes in sizes 3-15, as well as wigs and starlet lingerie. **McB's Shoes** (in Oakland, 546-9444) offers large size women's shoes for all you Bigfoot types looking for some decent heels.

WHEN I SAID I WANNA WATCH I DIDN'T MEAN A TIMEX

Ogle here, ogle there - if you like paying money to look at people, you'll find plenty of venues. If you want the listings complete with ratings of the venues and the strippers, visit www.tuscl.com, **The Ultimate Strip Club List**. You'll be able to find out which nights at which places are good for lap dances or live sex shows, what the cover prices are, and which dancers aren't to be missed. The venue web sites are also helpful.

If want to feast your eyes on dancing boys, check out the **New Meat Campus Theater** (220 Jones at Turk, 673-3384), **Nob Hill Cinema** (729 Bush at Powell, 781-9468), or the **Tea Room Theater** (145 Eddy at Taylor, 885-9887), which all offer a variety of performances or all-male films.

My straight male friends unanimously prefer the girls at the **Crazy Horse** (980 Market at 5th St., 771-6259, www.crazyhorse-sf.com). If you want to pay a lot of money to sit with Japanese businessmen, you can also try the **O'Farrell Theater** (895 O'Farrell at 12th St., 776-6686), which was started by SF's own Mitchell Brothers, the notorious pair who started the porn film industry as we know it.

The famously unionized peepshow at the woman-owned and operated **Lusty Lady** (1033 Kearny at Broadway, 391-3126) promotes itself as "clean, safe and fun," which makes it sound like any other video game arcade. They're always advertising for new girls in the back pages of the weeklies, so if you're strapped for cash, consider a few shifts behind glass. Sex is never without politics in San Francisco; check out www.eda.org, the **Exotic Dancers Alliance**, to find out how working girls organize.

I don't know whether the guys at the **Gold Club** (650 Howard at 3rd St., 536-0300) look like the guy in the ad, but apparently the girls look a lot better. **The New Century Theater** (816 Larkin, 776-3045) offers private showgirl "fantasy rooms."

THE ART OF SEX, THE SEX OF ART

If you like sex as subject matter, or kinky theatre, or silly people doing naughty things, you'll find company on the **Squid List** (www.laughingsquid.org), which lists all sorts of alternative art and culture events, including such recent gems as "The Frisky Frolics," "Rated X Fine Art Photography," "Porn-E-Oke," and a French grand guignol revival that included girls eating earthworms from each other's feet. Also keep your eyes peeled for **Stinky's Peep Show** and **In Bed With Fairy Butch**. Venues changes, but these two shows (straight and dyke, respectively) are worth watching wherever you find them.

Black Books (800-818-8823, www.blackbooks.com) publishes the bisexual lit mag Black Sheets, as well as their eponymous resource guides. They also host several very entertaining literary events a year. Not satiated? Check for event flyers at Good Vibrations and Stormy Leather.

HOOKING UP

Did I mention that San Franciscans like to have sex? I polled my friends to see how they proceed when priority number one is getting laid. Some folks take the traditional route to the nearest dive bar, where they make eye contact and say nice things instead of "Nice tits." If you want to pick up a bike messenger, try **Zeitgeist** (199 Valencia at Duboce, 255-7505). For hipsters, head to the **Latin American Club** (3286 22nd St. at Valencia, 647-2732). To pick up a yuppie, look for the dot-com party listings on **www.sfgirl.com**. I'm keeping my, um, friends' hangouts a secret.

After bars, the second choice was personals ads. The *Guardian* and the *Weekly* offer incredible variety: gay, straight, kinky, married, whatever, and their entertainment value might be enough. On the other hand, those who've tried the online personal thing seem to dig it. Apparently you can check boxes that indicate whether you're looking for a relationship, you want to try dating, or you're just seeking a cheap lay. Popular choices: **Yahoo Personals** (personals.yahoo.com), **Match.com** (www.match.com), and **SF Weekly Romance** (www.sfweekly.com).

One intrepid soul I know swears by the phone chat lines. Apparently if you call during the evening, you can find a date for the night to dance or go drinking with, and if you call around last call you can find a date for what's left of the night. Warning to sober people: most of these folks are tweaked on something. Check the back pages of the *Guardian* or the *Spectator*, and be aware that the same chat lines run many different ads with different phone numbers.

Girls usually talk free; guys usually have to pay.

Need someplace to take someone for a few minutes? Assuming home and car are unavailable, try **Grand Central Sauna and Hot Tubs** (15 Fell at Market, 431-1370). How about a bar for a secret rendezvous? **The Lone Palm** (22nd St. near Guerrero, 648-0109) is that one bar where you won't run into anyone you know.

STEPPING OUT

Private sex clubs generally require an invitation or membership. The first rule is, you do not talk about Sex Club. If you're itching to get into The Scene, the best way to meet people is by taking a class or attending an art event, as described earlier, and being upfront about the fact that you're a pervert looking to meet people like yourself.

The bathhouses may be (mostly) history, but queer sex clubs still abound. **Eros** (2051 Market at Church, 864-3767) offers warm, safe settings for fulfilling fantasies of anonymous torrid sex. Condoms are provided on the house. Eros does host the occasional mixed party, too.

Power Exchange (74 Otis at Gough, 487-9944, www.powerexchange.com) has separate entrances for men only or for women and couples. This cavernous space offers every cliché fantasy as its own room, from Victorian garden to post-apocalyptic to a replica of the gym. Check the Web site for special events, or just show up with your bag of tricks Thursday-Sunday after 9 p.m. **The Pleasure Zone** is a roaming sex and dance club that doesn't allow unescorted men, just women and couples (www.pleasurezone69.com). In the East Bay, the **Arena** is a private home with a hot tub and sex parties, also for women and couples (510-881-1138).

If you want to watch some decorative faux bondage, try the long-running **Bondage-A-Go-Go** at the Cat Club (1190 Folsom at 8th, 431-3332) on Wednesday nights. There are plenty of other goth clubs, but those don't feature flogging. For private dungeons, optional dominatrix extra, visit **www.castlebar.com**.

If you're at all perverted, or just curious, or you just have a thing for chaps, you cannot miss the **Folsom Street Fair**, every year on the last Sunday in September (www.folsomstreetfair.com). Beer and sunshine mix well with leatherclad dogs and spanking contests, and this is a great place to get all your holiday shopping done. My favorite item this year: a t-shirt reading "Let Go of My Ears, I Know What I'm Doing."

THE ICING ON THE CAKE

Some friends wanted a special birthday gift for our friend Larry, so they walked into the **Cake Gallery** (290 9th St. at Folsom, 861-CAKE) and described him, asking, "Can you make a cake with a picture of Larry sucking Satan's dick?" The astonishing likeness aside, the cake actually tasted great. Pick your body part or peruse their photo album.

Kinky San Francisco is lapping at your feet. We're just scratching the surface here, so pick a safeword, grab a newspaper or a Web browser - or even better, a partner - and dig in. You'll be glad you came.

BACKDOORS & SIDE ALLEYS
QUEER SAN FRANCISCO
BY MILES LONG

Like a lot of homos fresh off the farm, magnetically drawn to Sodom-by-the-Bay, I thought that San Francisco was a monolithically homocentric paradise waiting for me to pluck the many pleasures found on its every street corner. Think again. While there's plenty to see and do for the discerning dyke or hankerin' homo, much of it isn't visible to the naked eye. Take the Castro, for instance. Please!

My first visit to this shrine for queer pilgrims was like bad sex: is that all there is to it? It all seemed so depressingly normal, almost quaint, full of overpriced shops and bland tourist traps. So much for my starry-eyed, media-driven fantasies about a round-the-clock Mardi Gras atmosphere ladled evenly across San Francisco's 46 square miles. The center of the gay universe was just another yuppified, inbred urban enclave, as far as I could tell. I was relieved to discover, over the next few months, that there was much more to gay life in San Francisco than the Castro. I also learned that the Castro had more to offer than my first disappointing inspection proved.

CLOTHING: PASSION FOR FASHION

Most of the Castro's clothing stores are full of tacky boring knockoff threads at hyper-inflated prices sold by retail clerks with more attitude than Diana Ross. A few others, however, are worth the effort. You'll dazzle (or at least fit right in) walking down the lean mean streets of S.F. or Hollywood. But bear in mind such fashionable frocks might look a wee bit silly in Pittsburgh or Tulsa. Across palm-lined Market Street is **Crossroads** (2231 Market at 16th St., 626-8989; also 1901 Fillmore at Bush, 775-8885), which sells cool as fuck, mostly secondhand, jobs at very reasonable prices. They also buy, trade, and take some items on consignment. So it's a good bartering spot for those of us who, with more taste than money, are constantly updating our wardrobes.

For cheap, trendy togs, most younger fags & dykes, like their straight counterparts, go to Haight Street or the Mission for thrift stores or second-hand specialty shops. Always an experience. **Aardvarks** (1501 Haight at Ashbury, 621-3141) offers its own line of clothing, plus a plethora of used goods, especially denim, leather and brightly colored shirts & dresses. **Held Over** (1543 Haight at Ashbury, 864-0818) features a large selection of the usual fashion fare plus a lot of formal, forties, fifties and cowboy/girl drag. **Buffalo Exchange** (1555 Haight at Clayton, 431-7733; 1800 Polk at Washington, 346-5726) buys, sells and trades the latest Gen X garments. **Wasteland** (1660 Haight at Belvedere, 863-3150) is the largest of the Haight St. shops, with a little more variety and a stronger hip hop flavor to its general selection. **Villains** (1672 Haight at Belvedere, 626-5939) is also heavily hip hop, with a generous selection of leather, tee shirts and shoes. Both Villains and Wasteland are popular with visiting and local rock stars. Wow. While none of the Haight St. stores are specifically gay, a sizable percentage of their employees and customers are of the fruity persuasion.

The Mission, which I like to think of as the Castro's less affluent, more exciting Latino cousin, offers better buying grounds for poor white trash like myself, looking for those elusive bargains in this, one of the more expensive cities in the galaxy. **Clothes Contact** (473 Valencia at 16th St., 621-3212) offers clothes by the pound ($8, at last count). But the clerks often give you a discount if they think that's too much. **Community Thrift** (625 Valencia at 17th, 861-4910) is a gay-run charity, with most of its proceeds going to various gay and AIDS service organizations. Like most thrift stores, it sells everything besides clothing — housewares, music, furniture, bric-a-brac, books, videos, magazines, electronics. And like most thrift stores, it's really hit or miss what you find. Some days, it could be a great pair of boots for $7. Other days, nada. **The Salvation Army** (1509 Valencia at Cesar Chavez, 643-8040; 1185 Sutter at Polk, 771-3818) is a large, disorganized jungle of clothing and furniture, often worth the effort if you have the time to sift through their vast melange. I once completely outfitted myself for a wedding at this store for under $25. And I was among the nattier dressers at this august occasion, I might add. Rounding out the Mission cheapies is **Thrift Town** (2101 Mission at 17th St., 861-1132), among the largest secondhand emporia around these parts. Sadly, like many such shops in a town as trendy as ours, it often seems as if it has been picked clean, offering items that your grandmother probably wore five years ago. The best thing about Thrift Town is that they're constantly having sales to celebrate obscure holidays, such as Arbor Day or National Secretaries' Week. It's good to know that the silver lamé blouse you just bought is 30% off because George Washington & Abraham Lincoln both happened to be born in February. I love America!

Worn Out West (582 Castro at 19th St., 431-6020) is the store for those of us who get a kick outta walking in shitkickers and cowboy drag. Among the leather set, **Stormy Leather** (1174 Howard at 8th St., 626-1672) is popular among the younger crowd. Other homo leather stores include **A Taste of Leather** (1285 Folsom at 9th St., 252-9166).

DRINK & BE MERRY

For better or worse, bars are the center of gay culture. Like churches in the black community, they are social and political magnets. And while all the old-timers claim it ain't like it used to be, there are still more choices in S.F. than anywhere between here & the West Village or West Hollywood. **The Detour** (2348 Market at Castro, 861-6053) is a favorite neighborhood hangout in the Castro. With the cheapest beer, the darkest, tiniest interior, and the loudest music, it's bound to be interesting. Across the street is **The Cafe** (Market & Castro, 861-3846), still often referred to by its former name, Cafe San Marcos. This used to be considered the only women's bar in the Castro. And it was a good place for men to go who wanted to get away from the cruisey, hyper-male atmosphere in other local watering/glory holes. Unfortunately, word got out. Now, long, mostly male lines form outside on weekend nights, and the clientele seem to be 80% pushy, horny men. The last time I went there, it felt like a frat party. **The Mint** (1942 Market at Laguna, 626-4726) is a cute karaoke bar, which attracts a diverse crowd, often drunk before they even arrive. Sadly enough, most of the rest of the Castro bars don't even rate this high. They're all scary, tacky, slop troughs full of sweater queens and the usual slew of gay desperadoes and alcoholics. **The Pendulum** (4146 18th St. at Collingwood, 863-4441) could fit into this category, except that it is cheaper than most bars in the neighborhood, and is the only black gay bar that I know of in S.F. Its clientele is composed of near equal numbers of African-American men and their admirers.

Since this is a very cosmopolitan and racially diverse city, there are other gay bars that cater to different ethnic groups. **Esta Noche** (3079 16th St. at Mission, 861-5757) is famous for its Latino drag queens and strippers. It is rather small and seedy, and always packed. It can be quite fun. **The N Touch** (1548 Polk at California, 441-8413), located in the heart of one of the oldest gay neighborhoods in the country, is a gathering place for Asian men and their admirers. You know how us white men love to colonize. It offers karaoke and male strippers on various nights throughout the week. Not far away is **Diva's** (1081 Post at Polk, 928-6006), an infamous drag hangout that's been packin' 'em in for years.

If you like the rugged type, then head south, South of Market that is. **The Eagle** (398 12th St. at Harrison, 626-0880) has a real outdoorsy feel, with lots of biker & leather types lurking about. Every Sunday afternoon is an $8 beer bust. Beats the hell out of going to the park, eh? Down the street is **The Lone Star** (1354 Harrison at 9th St., 863-9999), a rough macho kind of place with peanut shells strewn on the floor, and men swilling beer & talking loudly to one another. Across the street is **The Stud** (399 9th St. at Harrison, 252-STUD), a legendary SF bar which has seen better days. Wednesday is Oldie's night, Monday's feature a tranny show and other nights offer various club adventures.

FOOD: EAT ME

Let's face it, after clothes & booze, there's nothing a self-respecting homo would want to waste his hard-earned money on besides food. And why not?! It's one of life's few reliable pleasures. In the town that knows how (to cook, that is), finding decent grub is no problem. I don't know about you, but when I shell out my shekels for someone else's food, I want a lot of bang for my buck. **La Mediterranee** (288 Noe at Market, 431-7210; also 2210 Fillmore at Sacramento, 921-2956) serves up Middle Eastern food to a mostly homo crowd. For dinner, come early (before 7 p.m.). The place is rather tiny and fills up fast. **Harvey's** (1582 Folsom at 12th St., 626-5767), with its funky decor and employees and proximity to nightclubs has been a perennial favorite of San Francisco's gay & lesbian community. But the prices are steep for their rather prosaic fare. Burger, fries, salad and a drink can run $16-22, an amount which used to feed me for a week when I was in school. Being the most nocturnal of creatures, queers dominate the late night food biz in SF, particularly in the center of town. **The Bagdad Cafe** (2295 Market at 16th St., 621-4434), **Orphan Andy's** (3993 17th St. at Market, 864-9795), and **Sparky's** (242 Church at Market, 621-6001) are all relatively inexpensive (if uninspiring) all night restaurants in the Castro-Upper Market area, frequented by fags & dykes of all stripes. **Hot & Hunky** (4039 18th St. at Castro, 621-6365) is sort of like a queer Burger King. I like to think of eating there as a metaphor for much of gay sex: quick, easy, cheap, and mostly pain- and guilt-free.

CLUBS: DANCING QUEENS

If there's one thing we queers are good at besides hairstyling, floral arranging, pet grooming & home decorating, it's shaking our thangs. Lots of the aforementioned bars offer dancing. But sometimes, you want the total club experience. You know: bitchy door thing; indifferent coat check wench; slow as molasses, moronic bartender; sadistic security personnel; and dumb as clams DJs playing the same annoying music all night long. Gee, I wonder why people do a lot of drugs in clubs? To get over the intense boredom most of these places generate, I would guess.

Don't mind me & my crabby rantings. There's plenty o' fun to be had for those willing to look. Bear in mind there's a high turnover in clubland. The names I write of here and now will more than likely change within a few months. The venues generally stay the same. So the important things to remember are the addresses. It seems as if about a half dozen or so spaces are used over and over for most of these ventures. A bit of advice: check out the record & clothing stores in the Castro for "invitation" cards to bars, clubs & parties. Most offer discounts on admission or even free admission before a certain hour.

Last call for alcohol in California is 2 a.m., which means they often shut off the bar by 1:30 and grab the drink out of your hand at 1:55. A lot of clubs stay open until 3 a.m. Some close as late as 4 a.m. and a few manage to stay open till dawn. These closing times seem to always be changing. So if you're planning on staying out late, find out the closing time in advance or ask at the door when you arrive. Most clubs are located South of Market, which is filling up with live/work lofts, whose occupants are continually whining to the city about their noisy neighbors. There is constant conflict between the clubs and the new cranky residents. Why don't these people just move to the suburbs?

The week starts out slow, everyone still recovering from the weekend's wantonness. On Mondays is **Joy** at **Liquid** (2925 16th St. at Mission, 431-8889, $4 cover), very young and crowded. Tuesdays is owned by **Trannyshack** at **The Stud** (399 9th St. at Harrison, 252-7883, $4 cover), a sexy, hilarious walk on the wild side with drag performances and dancing hosted by Heklina. The crowd is hot young boys & girls, flirty & friendly. Wednesdays offers **Cream** at **Butter** (354 11th St. at Folsom, 863-5964, $5 cover) full of cute kids slurping down cosmopolitans like the cocksuckers they are. It's a small, cool space with a circular bar and a big bathroom (perfect for that bootybump we all need). Thursdays brings **1984** (1190 Folsom at 8th St., 431-3332, $2 cover) with some of the finest male & female pulchritude this fair city has to offer. The crowd is mostly straight, but a lot of them look like they could go either way. The sound is very loud 80's dance music. **Reform Skool** (399 9th St. at Harrison, 252-7883, $5 cover) is usually pretty fun and always very trashy. It's the kind of place where the patrons start to disrobe along with the go-go dancers, after the third cocktail. Fridays is obviously a big night out in this small town that likes to shake its booty. And again, nearly all the action is South of Market. **Asia** (174 King at 3rd St., 974-6020, $10 cover) is every 2nd & 4th Fridays at King St. Garage. It's for young hot Asian dudes & their friends. **Fag Fridays** (401 6th St. at Harrison, 357-0827, $7 cover) is at the **End Up**, a boozy, cruisey, druggie journey into night. It stays open until 6 a.m., later than just about any other place around. **Club Q** (177 Townsend at 3rd St., 974-6020, $8 cover) is every first Friday at Townsend, the largest lesbian venue in SF. After recovering from the shakes and dry heaves, taking your disco nap and powdering your nose, it's time for some Saturday Night Fever. **Futura** (174 King at 3rd, $12 cover) is another space for Latinos and the men who love them, with lots of Spanish house music & other Latin styles. Muy caliente! **Girl Spot** (401 6th St. at

Harrison, $7 cover) is a chick thang at the End Up. **Universe** (177 Townsend at 3rd, 974-6020, $12 cover) still packs 'em in at Townsend with thousands of sweaty, shirtless, drug addled muscle boys dancing till dawn. Then there's **Sugar** (399 9th St. at Harrison, 292-7883, $8 cover) with lots o' boys & girls of all colors & ages (well, mostly in their 20's & 30's) who like to have fun. The crowd is pretty, hip & ready to party, which ends at 4 a.m.

After you're done resting and repenting, the party starts up again on Sunday. **T Dance** at End Up (401 6th St. at Harrison, 357-0827, $5 cover) feels like a continuation of the other weekend clubs there: lots of young, strangely energetic kids who love to dance. **Sixxteen** (1190 Folsom, 431-3332, $5 cover) is a trashy, mostly straight (but queer friendly) venue with rock & roll from the 70's & 80's. That completes our tour of San Francisco's queer clubland. Now take a pill and sleep it off.

STREET BEAT

There are numerous festivals and street fairs during the summer and fall with a queer bent. First up is **Gay Pride**, which is generally held over the last weekend in June to commemorate the Stonewall riot in 1969. Nothing official happens on Friday, but the streets, bars and clubs are packed. Make sure to book early. This is usually the busiest, most crowded week of the year in one of the world's biggest tourist destinations. On Saturday, there is the **Dyke March**, starting at Dolores Park (19th at Dolores) around 7 p.m. Later in the evening, the Castro is blocked off for a huge street party. Everyone seems to be drunk or on drugs, stumbling and slobbering. It can actually get tedious after a while. Make sure you're with people who don't bore you, or find them quick. Because if you haven't found a party, you'll probably do a lot of walking and drinking. On Sunday is the parade, which travels down Market Street, usually from the Embarcadero to the Civic Center. It is massive, with the crowds estimated at anywhere from 200,000 to 500,000. After the parade, around 1 p.m. or so, is the huge celebration at the Civic Center. Bring water, sunblock and other supplies (breathmints, condoms, lube) that might come in handy. It's gonna be a long day.

Next up is **Dore Alley Fair**, a rather small but rowdy S&M/Leather party held in **Dore Alley** (between 9th & 10th, Folsom & Howard) during the third Sunday in July. Lots of flesh, a lot of booze. You know the drill.

The last Sunday in September brings **Folsom Street Fair**, the grand master of S&M street parties. It's quite huge, with tens of thousands of people crowding onto Folsom between 7th and 12th Streets. It sometimes looks like a fetish amusement park, with tourists resembling your parents getting their photos taken of themselves in cages or on racks. But overall, it's the real deal-another great excuse to get drunk and practice sexual deviance.

The following Sunday, the first in October, is the **Castro Street Fair**, another mass debauch. But after the festivities of the previous weekend, this one can seem like an anticlimax. The best thing about these two fairs is that they are held during the warmest and sunniest time of the year in San Francisco.

The days grow shorter and the nights cooler, and we mark the end of summer with one last exhibitionist extravaganza. **Halloween** is to SF what Mardi Gras is to New Orleans or Spring Break to Daytona Beach. The Castro is blocked off for another giant party. In recent years, the scene has gotten out of hand. Thousands pour in from outlying neighborhoods and the suburbs, as well as from far away. Some of them seem to be looking for trouble. There have been numerous arrests for assaults, shootings, stabbings, disorderly conduct, etc. Then the city decided to move the celebration to the Civic Center. But thankfully, the party in the Castro continues. Now, the thugs tend to go to the Civic Center and the beautiful people head to the Castro. The show must go on.

SEX

It is said that San Francisco is recession-proof because our main industries are food and sex. And there are a lot of hungry people out there, no? What to do when you've got a hankerin' for a hunk o' beef or a furburger? Never fear. Crack your cat o' nine tails in this town and you're bound to graze some flesh peddler.

For gay men seeking printed material of prurient interest, there's **Jaguar Books** (4057 18th St. at Castro, 863-4777) in the heart of the Castro, specializing in magazines, calendars and sex toys. **Le Salon** (1124 Polk), a famous purveyor of male porn, offers a large selection of videos (some of the vintage 70's variety), and magazines (including European smut). **The Magazine** (920 Larkin at Geary, 441-7737) offers all sorts of old porn (gay, straight, specialty) dating back to the 50's. If you want in the flesh action, check out the **Campus Theater** (220 Jones at Turk, 673-3384), **Nob Hill Cinema** (729 Bush at Stockton, 781-9468), or the **Tea Room Theater** (145 Eddy at Mason, 885-9887), which all offer a variety of performances, either live strip or jack-off shows, appearances by today's bigger porn stars or all-male fuck flicks. **Good Vibrations** (1210 Valencia at 23rd, 974-8980) is the infamous sex shop by women, for women, and mostly about women. Unlike some male-dominated establishments of this nature, however, the opposite gender is certainly welcome here. It is home to a variety of sex toys, gay & straight porn & erotica, and sex information.

For those seeking the comfort of strangers in a strange town, sex clubs are making a comeback as we near the end of the second decade of AIDS. **Power Exchange** (74 Otis at Gough, 487-9944), and **Eros** (2051 Market at Church, 864-3767), provide warm safe settings for cheap torrid sex with that special someone you'll never see again. **City Entertainment** (960 Folsom at 5th, 543-2124), **Frenchy's** (1020 Geary at Polk, 776-5940), and **Folsom Gulch** (947 Folsom at 5th, 495-6402) are all run of the mill porno stores infamous for the gay male action in their peep show booths.

For those who want their carnal thrills al fresco, San Francisco provides a cornucopia of outdoor pickup spots. **Collingwood Park** (19th St. & Collingwood, one block west of Castro) is synonymous with gay male sex. One recent warm evening when I happened to be strolling by en route to an indoor assignation (honest!), I witnessed scores of leering men of all ages, shapes and sizes, seeking to slake their lonely thirsts after one of those rare hot days in this cool gray city of love.

Buena Vista Park (Haight & Baker) and **Corona Heights** (Roosevelt & 16th St., one block west of Castro) are neighboring hills, the yin & yang of gay cruising spots. Buena Vista is leafy & lush, a sumptuous, steep climb several hundred feet up above Haight Street, with a panoramic view of the Pacific Ocean, Golden Gate Bridge, downtown and the bay. You'll work those leg muscles as you view the male fauna in his predatory mode. Buena Vista consists mostly of men over 35 with mustaches, walking their dogs (a universally popular ruse among cruisers). Corona Heights, just a block away, is smaller but more rugged, a stark, barren outcropping of stone overlooking the gay center of town. The crowd here tends to be younger and more adventurous. You have to be to make the sometimes-treacherous ascent to the top.

South of Market, San Francisco's clubland, with its density of male dominated leather and sex bars, is home to two famous sex alleys. **Dore Alley** (between Howard & Folsom, 9th & 10th) has its own S & M oriented summer fair. **Ringold Alley** (between Folsom & Harrison, 8th & 9th) is more legend than fact at this point. Both of these places, victims of changing times, police crackdowns, AIDS and neighborhood complaints, probably saw more action in years past.

Polk Street, the old heart of gay San Francisco, is now home to Southeast Asian immigrants and teenage hustlers. With lots of gay bars and sex shops, it is a magnet for troubled young runaways and the men who are attracted to them. This is not so much a pickup spot as a flesh market. Expect to pay for this tender veal. Other famous cruising spots include **JFK Drive** in Golden Gate Park, near Ocean Beach (automobile-oriented, lots of older, married types), **Land's End**, above Cliff House (a nocturnal phenomenon, can be Dangerous), and **Golden Gate Beach**, in the Presidio (a steep descent from the parking lot, clothing optional, extremely gay).

ALL THE WORLD'S A STAGE

There are a variety of theaters and performance spaces for homolesbos in San Francisco. Some are queer-specific. Others are just queer-friendly.

For movie houses, the obvious choice is the **Castro Theater** (429 Castro at 19th, 621-6120), the grand old dowager of old style theaters, with an 80 foot ceiling, a giant chandelier, a Wurlitzer and real live piano player to go along with it, that ascend and descend on a circular platform to and from the orchestra pit. The Castro Theater is home base for the **San Francisco Gay & Lesbian Film Festival** every June. The **Roxie Cinema** (3117 16th St. at Valencia, 863-

1087) is another venue for the film festival. While the Castro shows more classics loved by gay audiences (*All About Eve*, *Valley of the Dolls*), and a lot of queer cinema, the Roxie tends to show film noir, violent action flicks and more experimental independent films.

For performances geared toward gay & lesbian audiences, **Theater Rhinoceros** (2940 16th St. at Mission, 861-5079) is a homo-run playhouse that presents original performances, often featuring local queer talent. Across the street is the **Victoria Theater** (2961 16th St., 863-7576), which is open sporadically, offering its fair share of queer plays, cabaret acts & musical reviews. Other performance spaces of interest to the gay & lesbian audience (depending on the work of the moment) include the **Lab** (2948 16th St. at Mission, 864-8855), **Artist's Television Access**, or ATA (992 Valencia at 21st St., 824-3890), **Theater Artaud** (450 Florida at 17th, 621-7797), a live/work/performance salon, **Intersection for the Arts** (446 Valencia, at 15th St., 626-3311), **Jon Sims Performing Arts Center** (1519 Mission, 554-0402) and the **Queer Cultural Center** (1800 Market, 552-7709).

ART GALLERIES

This is familiar territory for many urban fags & dykes, especially in San Francisco, where everyone fancies himself or herself an artiste or performer of some sort. I'm not even going to deal with most of the big downtown galleries, where art is a commodity to be bought and sold by a tiny elite, or with stores that call themselves galleries, but in reality just sell softcore homoerotica. No, let's talk about the handful of places, some serious, some more whimsical, which actually trade in ideas and objects of interest to all sorts of queers. **Southern Exposure** (401 Alabama at 17th, 863-2141) is a neato alternative gallery with some impressive work at times, and enough clout to gain a measure of credibility. Other interesting galleries with a queer bent (to varying degrees) include **New Langton Arts** (1246 Folsom at 8th, 626-5416), and **Minna Street Gallery** (111 Minna at 2nd St. 974-1719). **The Keane Eyes Gallery** (3036 Larkin, 922-9309), while not queer-oriented, is the home base for perhaps San Francisco's most famous painter, Margaret Keane. She, of course, is the progenitor of those large-eyed waifs, the fashionable icon of our youth-obsessed times. Other non-queer specific places of interest in the art world include the **Cartoon Art Museum** (655 Mission at 3rd, 227-8666) and the **Frankel Gallery** (49 Geary at Kearny, 981-2661), part of a complex of upscale galleries, the kind I promised not to mention earlier. Sorry. But it's so good, I had to.

MISCELLANY

A Different Light bookstore (489 Castro at Market, 431-0891) is the Library of Congress for West Coast queer culture. It has it all, from coffee table volumes on supermodels to esoteric sociological studies. It is always crowded, morning, noon & night, and is the place to see & hear local or visiting gay & lesbian writers. **Bound Together** (1369 Haight at Masonic, 431-8355) is a really cool anarchist book collective. They're very good with alternative queer material. Another favorite of mine is a cavernous used bookstore called **McDonald's** (48 Turk at Market, 673-2235), which bills itself as "A Dirty, Poorly Lit Place for Books." What more could you want?

Leather Tongue Video (714 Valencia at 18th, 552-2900) has one of the best selections of way-out, hard to find videos. And it is also sells comics and zines. Modern primitives seeking new metal thrills go to **Body Manipulations** (3234 16th St. at Guerrero, 621-0408).

For very gay friendly (and cheap) accommodations the Castro, there's **Beck's Motor Lodge** (2222 Market at 15th, 621-8212). It's the perfect spot for an assignation or a small among your new friends during Gay Pride Weekend or Castro Street Fair. The rooms are clean and pleasant, but also bland and cheesy in that Motel 6 sort of way. They look like the set of some '90s porno movie. Outside, along the corridors, a lot of the patrons keep their curtains open and their doors ajar, lounging in their undergarments or strolling around the grounds. It's quite easy to make new friends in this sort of environment. In the Polk Street area, there's the **Phoenix Hotel** (601 Eddy at Polk, 776-1380), which is popular with visiting rock stars. The Phoenix has a fashionable restaurant and nightspot called Backflip, which is popular with the young martini set. I've been to some fun parties there. But it might not be everyone's cup of tea.

TENDERLOIN BAR CRAWL
BY SPIKE

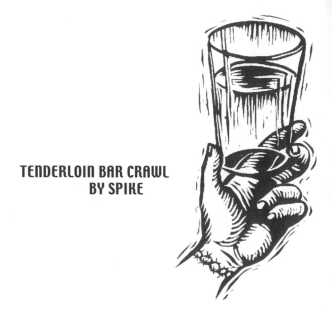

*****God drinks here ****Outstanding ***Worth the trip
**O.K. if you're really thirsty *Skip it

Aging ex-service men tell humbling tales of wartime glory and postwar debauchery. Jaundiced, gin blossomed old drunks deliver bar stool sermons with time delayed bits of infinite wisdom. Somber jaded queens reminisce about youth, home, and Harvey Milk. Outside, there are violent shrieks and stifled cries, but Cookie welcomes you at the door with a handshake and a smile and the contrast is blinding. A columnist for a punk rock magazine reads one too many Beat novels and writes a pretentious intro... wouldn't you?

The Tenderloin. Nothing tender about it, pal. It's fabled

that it earned its name almost a century ago, when the police who patrolled this squalid area earned extra hazard pay. These cops could therefore afford the choicer cuts of meat, the tenderloins. These days, any shmoe with fifty bucks, a hard dick and a strong stomach can afford everything he needs and hours of it.

It is our city within a city. Sober, I have never felt entirely safe in the Tenderloin; but drink by drink the TL's womblike spell has put me in a fuckin' vice grip every time.

Mike, Jerry, Darv, Antoine, and I recently set out to dispel any and all current myths circulating about this misunderstood area. Later, dim recollections, photos, and Mike's extensive notes were our only reference point to document our departure from sanity into a nether world of smoky bars, neon signs, and transvestite prostitutes. And hopefully this will serve as an indispensable travel guide to both residents and visitors to our fair city.

Our first stop was the **Club Charleston** (10 6th St. at Market and Mission, 431-0544*****) and the bartender's name was Joe. Joe wouldn't and still won't accept tips under any circumstances. "Save it for when we raise the drink prices," he said. My hat goes off to this man.

Maybe it was the shape of the bar or its blinking neon sign, maybe the honest eyes and kind words of the bartender named Joe. Come to think of it though, it was probably the t-shirt pinned above the bar with EVERYTHING DIES emblazoned on the front. I don't know but I've grown very fond of this place in a few short visits, so I'd appreciate it if you took your dreadlocks and pierced lips somewhere else. You wouldn't understand.

On to **Aunt Charlie's** (133 Turk at Taylor/Full Bar, 441-2922***) How can you go wrong with a place that has a peach and pink interior? You get the impression that broken-down old queens that were exiled from the Castro and never made it on Polk Street end up here. Mike watched as two elderly gentlemen argued about who had a facelift and who didn't, but I didn't want to hear about it.

I stumbled upon the jukebox and entirely by accident found "Needle and the Spoon" by Skynyrd and "When I'm 64" from *Sgt. Pepper*. How could I have imagined how appropriate my musical selections would prove to be? Kit from the Peter Pan showed up wearing a new leather vest that said RAMROD in studs on the back, and generally ignored us. I know how to take a hint.

In keeping with this night of mind numbing contrasts, we decided to haul our asses from that pit of "koks" straight into that urban isle of whisky drinkin', potato eatin' macho misery: **Harrington's Pub** (460 Larkin at Turk, 775-1150***1/2). With tables lined up in the middle of the joint like lunch time at the Stuttering County Fair, this barely lit bar appealed strangely to my barely Irish sensibilities. An ill-tempered man behind the bar wearing an IRELAND t-shirt introduced himself. "Me name's Patty!"— oh god, here it comes— "What?...Paddy?" Mike asked innocently enough. "PATTY!" our bartender bellowed. "Short fer Patrick!" After briefly lecturing Mike on Irish slurs and common responses, I ordered a whisky with a beer behind it, and quietly took stock in my surroundings. There wasn't much to distract me from my drink, so drink I did. But mid-beer I was interrupted.

"CLOSIN' TIME," shouted Paddy. What!? It wasn't even midnight! Patrick softened the blow by giving us all green drink chips, "Good fer a drink anytime-BUT NAY TONIGHT!" We got the picture and got up to leave. On our way out he invited us in for lunch. "WE GOT BOILED CABBAGE!" Aye.

The next place I've passed on my way home quite a few times, but never thought twice about actually entering.

Anyhow, Jerry boldly led us through the swinging doors of the **Brown Jug Saloon** (496 Eddy at Hyde, 441-8404/Full Bar****) We landed quite by accident at a birthday party, the likes of which I had never seen. The bash was being thrown for a woman who, incidentally, once propositioned me on the street. We found a spot at the bar, ordered $1.00 glasses of Miller, and watched in quiet awe as a drunken group of people tried unsuccessfully to form a straight conga line. This lasted less than a minute until one balding gimp in a nehru jacket broke away and danced spastically by the jukebox, eventually collapsing into the arms of the other revelers. Fuck, I didn't know whether to feel smug or jealous.

I could have been mistaken but all eyes in the bar seemed to be staring at us, and these were more than friendly stares. The party was over, and again we had work to do.

Come no further than **Jonell's** (401 Ellis at Jones, 776-8345/Full Bar-Strong cheap drinks!****) for your last history lesson. A woman behind the bar wearing a Sturgis t-shirt enthusiastically beckoned us inside, so we sidled up to the bar and ordered our first round. The actual bar was set up like a sort of U-shaped feeding trough, which made for an interesting visual effect. John, one of the people hungrily 'feeding' there introduced himself. "This place was once classy, I made it classy." John chose Jerry for the obligatory ear-bending. "See ya, Jerry". I on the other hand, moved over to the corner that was less crowded, so drinks could be more easily ordered. Already seated there was a British woman in her mid-70s wearing a lavish bright red outfit which, she later revealed, was of her own design. She spoke with an almost aristocratic—if somewhat slurred—English accent, and in a low scratchy scotch-soaked voice. My new friend Kathleen began to tell me stories from her life in Britain during the Second World War, pausing occasionally to pinch my cheeks and compliment my boyish looks. When

I told her that my grandfather was a decorated General back then, some asshole sitting next to her suddenly said, "A General, huh?...What the hell happened to you?" I was caught off guard and didn't respond, so he went on with more war stories, this time from Vietnam. I had a war on either side of me.

Then suddenly, a pug-nosed drunk with an upturned baseball cap put me in a bear hug and kissed me on the cheek. "I'm a hobbies investigator," he boasted. "Wanna see my badge?" He flashed me a beat up old business card with a star and some writing on it, and then sat back down.

We sat for awhile with our new friends, and as the time flew by so did the whisky and beer, and I eventually found myself at a table with Mike, drunkenly reasserting dominance over my wife. "FROM NOW ON, I WEAR THE FUCKIN' PANTS AROUND HERE...GET IT?...ME!" Sorry, Katja.

Right in the middle of my soliloquy, Kathleen called me aside. "I want you to see how I live, young man," she said, asking me to escort her home. I was being hit on. I politely refused, explaining that I had work to do. She kissed me goodnight, stumbled and spilled Mike's beer right into his lap. Then, regaining her composure, she strode elegantly to the door.

Back at the bar, I tried to engage the Vietnam guy in some small talk, but he just scowled disgustedly at me.

"I know you're a hustler, you know you're a hustler, and any damn fool who takes you home better watch his wallet." I couldn't believe it! First, some cretinous cowboy kisses me with his eyes closed, then I'm branded a whore by a West Point dropout! So long Jonell's, I didn't even bother denying it.

Right across the street was our last stop, the **Cinnabar** (397 Ellis at Jones, 928-4288/Way Full Bar***). Things were getting pretty cloudy by now. The bartender's name was Paula, and after we told her what we had been up to, she told us that she had worked in almost every bar we had been in. Anytime anyone's name was mentioned in the context of alcohol, she would say, "He was totaled." So being that it was 1:30 a.m., that became the big word for the rest of the evening. Everyone in the place was either shooting pool for money or playing poker machines really hard. I think I did a little of both. One thing's for sure, I don't remember going off on Middle Eastern men, until Mike played a tape of me shouting obscenities in the men's room the next day.

Well, somehow we all made it home, and I slept for the next sixteen hours. I guess it's true what some people say, "The Good Lord always watches over drunks." Hey, where's my fuckin' hazard pay?

THE MISSION AIN'T WHAT IT USED TO BE
BY BUCKY SINISTER

The Mission ain't what it used to be. If you hang out in this neighborhood for more than an hour, chances are you'll hear someone say this. One of the favorite conversations of us locals is how the neighborhood has changed, how it's horrible now, how it's damn near unlivable, how each moment is unbearable agony, and goddess help us if we have to move because we could never stand to live anywhere else. Thing is, with this neighborhood, it always ain't what it used to be.

This neighborhood has changed hands more often than the town glove. Dozens of demographic groups have laid claim to this neighborhood over the last fifty years. There's a structure that's somewhat stable insofar as streets are concerned, but the rest of the businesses, inhabitants, and activities are due to change at any moment. As soon as empty space opens, it is filled with someone or something newer. Fifteen years ago, there were hardly any cafes in the Mission. Seven years ago, there were twice as many as there are now. Ten years from now, the same will be true of yoga studios. There were once secondhand and thrift stores all over the place; now there are upscale furniture boutiques filled with refurbished furniture from the former businesses. The vacant warehouse spaces once home to underground clubs that were shut down to make room for internet businesses are vacant again: that is, they look exactly as they did twelve years ago. The only consistency this neighborhood has is the proliferation of drugs and prostitutes.

Oh, the places you'll go! From the Latin drag queens of Esta Noche to the Folsom Street crackheads, there's all manner of trouble to get into and endless ill advice to be taken. There's an underground in this neighborhood that, if you wanted to be a part of, you probably wouldn't be a book reading type. So for your sake, here are some fun places to go and great things to do in the Mission without ruining your life. One more word of advice to tourists: thieves here will steal anything at all, so leave your DV cam in the hotel safe, take public transit instead of the rental car, and when people offer to sell you an outfit, they mean a syringe, spoon, and rubber tie-off.

Theater Spanganga (19th St. at Mission) - Run by local comedians for comedians, this theater space is liable to have any kind of a show, from sketch comedy to music. Check out local comics working out their new acts, and improv groups who still think improvisation can be funny.

Hot Dog Carts (on the street: try 16th St. & Valencia or 23rd St. & Mission)- Not only are the wieners great, but there's a slice of bacon wrapped around every one. Top it with some grilled onions and mayonnaise, and you've got all the fat you need for two days in one easy snack.

Muddy Waters (521 Valencia at 16th St., 863-8006; 1304 Valencia at 24th St., 647-7994) - There's two of these on either end of Valencia Street. Their coffee has claws. Do yourself a favor and get a small and have it watered down if you're not of a profession like a NASCAR driver or something where you're used to your heart beating near top capacity for hours at a time.

Taquerias: **El Farolito** (Mission at 24th St., 337-5500) Their super quesadilla suiza is a cheese delivery system. **Cancun** (Mission at 19th St.) has the best carne asada burrito in town. **El Castillito** (Mission at 17th St.) open really late till bars' closing time. A burrito is the size of a child's arm. A super burrito is the size of your arm. "With jalapenos," means lots of fresh, very active jalapenos.

Places with **Chinese food and Doughnuts** (Mission at 24th St.) - They use the same fryer for both. Cruellers taste like Kung Pao Chicken, and egg rolls taste like buttermilk bars. This is surprisingly pleasing.

MY FAVORITE MISSION BARS AND BARTENDERS

There are too many bars to mention them all. At the risk of filling up my favorite bars with tourists, here goes.

Dalva (3121 16th St. at Valencia, 252-7740) - This bar has poetry open mikes every other Thursday. The Mission once had open mikes almost every night of the week. Bring your journal. Read a poem. Even if it sucks, you're not going to be in town long.

Amnesia (853 Valencia at 19th St., 970-8336) This used to be the Chameleon. It's pretty much the same bar but they clean the bathrooms and pay the bills.

Baobab (3388 19th St. 643-3558) West African cuisine with a full bar. They have a slew of cocktails made with ginger that are unlike any cocktail anywhere else.

Doc's Clock (2575 Mission at 21st St., 824-3627) The sign! Oh my god! The best bar sign I've ever seen in my life. It's from the era when this part of Mission Street was known as The Miracle Mile.

The Kilowatt (3160 16th St. at Valencia, 861-2595) Two pool tables with plenty of action. A good place to go for Sunday football games.

Sadie's (491 Potrero at Mariposa, 551-7988) Numerous couches, free popcorn, cheap cocktails, pool, and pinball. What more could you ask for? The first Sunday of the month it is the home of Kvetch, an all queer open mike.

The Uptown (200 Capp at 17th St., 861-8231) The first time I went in here and ordered a double bourbon and coke, they made it in a pint glass. That made me a repeat customer.

Zeitgeist (199 Valencia at Duboce, 255-7505) This bar has a patio, which means you can smoke while you drink. What a concept! The pint-sized Bloody Marys are recommended.

Sacrifice Bar and Grill (800 South Van Ness at 19th St., 641-0990). Starting at 4 p.m. Monday through Friday until 7 p.m., happy hour is two for one cocktails. I can't stress this enough. This is the only real drink bargain in the Mission if you're into drinking anything other than well drinks.

The Lexington Club (3464 19th St. at Mission St., 863-2052) Where every night is ladies' night. It's a dyke bar. I'm including this so our dyke readers will know where to get their drink on in a primarily straight neighborhood. Please, straight people, if you want to be touristy and see real live lesbians, go to Home Depot.

Mission Records (2263 Mission at 18th St., 285-1550) One of the few new places in the neighborhood with the old flavor. Punk as fuck. There are shows in the back room some afternoons. The smelliest place in the world to see a band.

They also buy and sell records and CDs.

Community Thrift (623 Valencia at 17th St., 861-4910) Still nonprofit, still liable to have anything, including things of yours you haven't seen since Mom sold it at a garage sale in the '90s A good place to go for a cheap coat if for some reason you thought it would be over sixty degrees in California in June.

Red Dora's Bearded Lady (485 14th St. at Valencia, 626-2805) This is a dyke owned and operated café. Not too long ago, there were many stores and businesses in the neighborhood that were part of a thriving lesbian community.

Abandoned Planet (518 Valencia at 16th St., 861-4695) What sets this bookstore apart are the ever-present Bukowski collectibles.

OTHER COOL MISSION STUFF

Anarchist Emma Goldman lived at 569 Dolores in 1916. 24th Street is home to some really rad happenings.

Balmy Alley is a block-long Latino muralfest, an unrivalled display of public, community-based art. U2 shot one of their videos there a million years ago.

Clarion Alley (between Mission & Valencia) has murals by some of SF's best-loved underground comix artists like Matso, Keith Knight, and Greta Snyder.

Buy good luck candles and supplies for casting magic spells at **Botanica Yoruba** (998 Valencia at 21st St., 826-4967).

Fresh tortillas are made by hand daily at **La Palma Mexicatessen** (2884 24th St. at Florida, 647-1500).

The salsa at **Casa Sanchez** (2778 24th St. at Treat St., 282-2400) rules!

THE LOST MISSION
BY YOLANDA MONTIJO

The hour inevitably comes when you wonder, perhaps out loud, perhaps after a drink or three, preferably a martini with three olives, and preferably at **Doc's Clock** (2575 Mission St. near 22nd, 824-3627, just look for the neon arch), where the hell does Mission Street end? Or does it? Do streets always have to end and when they do, wouldn't it be nice if they could end somewhere in San Angel, Baja Mexico? Still, if you haven't found your street to Baja, then surely the Mission district and the Outer Mission are the next best thing. And if you're on Mission Street and can make it past 26th Street, just when or where you thought it was all over and time to turn back, well, don't, instead cross Cesar Chavez and you're delivered with no fanfare into my world; the Outer Mission, the Lost Mission, Baja Mission, the closest you'll come to Almost Mexico without leaving the city.

HOW DO I GET LOST?

Who can say where the Outer Mission begins or ends, though it may be safe to venture that if you've gone too far south down Mission Street and wonder where the hell you are, then you've found it. Just like that. Or get off at the 24th Street BART stop and go south. Just after you pass Cesar Chavez on Mission Street, you may not notice the remarkably plain, former Sears building, now converted into live/work lofts (whose inhabitants include the people who bring you He'Brew Beer and one MacArthur Fellowship recipient; two separate people). Directly after the Sears building, you'll find the bright purple facade of **Roccapulco** (3140 Mission St. at Cesar Chavez 648-6611), one of the liveliest and largest, generally latin dance clubs in the city. Major latin and sometimes lesser, but still excellent rock/ hip-hop bands, often headline weekend shows, creating long lines of excited, coiffed and heavily cologned scenesters. Just look for the extra short skirts. A great place to cruise by should you own a black '67 Riviera.

ONCE I'M LOST WHAT CAN I EAT?

More importantly than whether you've come accidentally or purposefully, always bring your appetite. And at least four bucks. Make that twenty.

First the gods cut you some slack and you find affordable housing, then you ask, still talking to yourself here, where the hell am I supposed to get my coffee? Fortunately, our answer was almost next door. **Cafe Commons** (3161 Mission St. at Cesar Chavez, 282-2928), owned and run by one of the nicest couples anywhere, is a clean, lively coffeehouse, with a great deck and ample outdoor seating. Oversatisfies all your coffee needs. Lush sandwiches, homemade gourmet soups (the cheddar corn chowder is a lesser known deity), and bagels with all the proper fixings; our favorite being lox, cream cheese, and tomatoes ($5), the best cure for anything that happened Saturday night.

Then, there's my truly underground aboveground favorite restaurant**, Emmy's Spaghetti Shack** (18 Virginia St. at Mission, 206-2086, open everyday 6pm-midnight, F & Sat 6 p.m.-2 a.m.) 1. Full bar. 2. Dark sexy lighting. 3. Spaghetti and meatballs: $7.50. 4. DJs/live music. 5. Sweet & saucy waitstaff. Love everything about this place.

Taqueria Cancun (3211 Mission at 29th St., 550-

1414). The infamous, loglike Cancun vegetarian burrito is the closest you'll come to a faithful friend you can eat; always there, always filling. As soon as you order anything, you're given the red basket or bag-to-go of chips with two kinds of salsa; our favorite being the tangy salsa verde. Plus $1 agua frescas, cheap Mexican beers, and excellent nachos (never order them to go unless you have an extra hour to kill). Everyone in the hood comes here.

For the more traditional sit-down, less taqueria atmosphere, try **Brisas De Acapulco** (3137 Mission St. at Army, 826-1496). The interior is spare cafeteriaesque, but the food is all authentic Mexican/Salvadorian. Highly recommended is the enchiladas verdes plate (big stuffed enchiladas, thick refried beans, rice and salad), a "bahgin" at $7.95. **El Patio** (3193 Mission St. at Valencia, 641-5056) is another good, affordable Mexican/Salvadorian restaurant, with, we assume, an outdoor patio (though we've not seen it). A very lively place, and right next door to an even livelier, small evangelical church, this restaurant has an extensive menu of traditional and perhaps more exotic fare. These are some of our favorites of the neighborhood Mexican/Salvadorian restaurants, but be adventurous, try a different place; our rule of thumb is, if there are healthy looking people inside, we'll give it a chance.

One of the best kept secrets in the Mission, if not the city, is **Blue Plate** (3218 Mission St. at 29th St., 282-6777). Enter through the humble brick exterior and you find a beautiful, eclectically decored front room with a lush red back parlor, serving American classics with the right California twist. Gorgeous entrees ($13 & up), incredible appetizers and salads ($6 & up), and a great wine list. Our favorites include the meatloaf, anything with mashed potatoes, and the mizuna salad with jewel-like bits of blue cheese and candied walnuts (the taste of the vinaigrette alone brings tears).

Whether we get up in time for breakfast or not on the weekend, or don't get up at all, thankfully there's **Al's Cafe Good Food** (3286 1/2 Mission St. at 29th St., 641-8445, open daily at 7 a.m.). Breakfast is served anytime, and while the good may come and go, it's always hot, plentiful, and cheap. Big plate of sausage & eggs with home fries and toast: $5.95. Think old-fashioned diner food and "whatall ya have, honey" waitresses but without the parking. Al has also covered his walls with every old Hollywood star imaginable and the kitschy seasonal front window display rivals Macy's any day.

Pad Thai Restaurant (3259 Mission St. 29th St., 285-4210), though not so poetic in name, is our choice for neighborhood Thai chow, with the usual reliably tasty mix of Thai curries, coconut milk soups, and hot seafood dishes. We love the traditional Tom Kha Jay soup; a spicy, coconut milky, delicately flavored soup (works the same on colds as matzoh ball or chicken soup). And if you can't leave the house, but desire Thai food (it happens), then they even offer free delivery ($10 minimum), 5-10 p.m., everyday except Wednesday, when, for some reason known only to them, they're closed.

WHERE EVERY DRINK IS SPECIAL

In Greek mythology, bear with me here, Argus was the giant with a hundred eyes who was made guardian of Io, but later slain by Hermes. The name alone came to imply a watchful person, a guardian, and it's great to find a whole bar embodying that in both name and spirit. **Argus Lounge** (3187 Mission St. at Valencia, 824-1447, closed Mondays, www.arguslounge.com) is our other living room; the small, beautiful, red-and-mint walled neighborhood bar of our dreams. It's with some reluctance and in spite of threats from friends and even myself, that I share it. From the fishnet lights lacing the walls to the cow skulls and mammoth angry clown painting, Argus serves excellent and often brimming drinks by great bartenders we know and love (Amy, Jenny, Josh, Paul). The jukebox rocks and pool is only 50 cents. There's no name outside, just look for the bright peacock's eye sign.

Odeon Bar (3223 Mission St. at Valencia St., 550-6994) lies just down the street from Argus. Owned and run by local art-man-around-town Chicken John, the newly revamped Odeon Bar now hosts an eclectic 'weakly' mix of musique, curio, and just damn unordinary events, where anything goes and usually does. Still, a good neighborhood bar. Very cool collection of antique wind-up toys behind the bar.

Go one block further south, and you'll hit **Keane's 3300 Club** (3300 Mission St. at 29th St., 826-6886, www.3300club.com). In business for half a century now, Keane's 3300 Club is an establishment, a classic if not legendary old Irish bar with a true poetic bent. The smell of history practically punches you in the face as you walk in. Poetry readings held two nights a month. Call or check out their website for the poetry schedule.

Your real dive bar is the great **El Rio** (3158 Mission St. at Valencia, 282-3325, www.elriosf.com), home and host to a diverse, truly San Francisco variety of dance parties, live bands, film series, dance groups, and more. Support El Rio alone as a venue for a great mix of live music, with everything from salsa, East Indian, and African to indie rock and rockabilly. The place is sprawling, and has a separate bar with pool table (sometimes mysteriously free), a huge, tropical outdoor patio, and a back room for live music. If you go for the live music, get there a bit early and ruthlessly stake out a space near the stage in the back room, otherwise if there's a crowd, all you see is hair.

26 Mix (3024 Mission at 26th St., closed Mondays, 248-1319, www.26mix.com) has come into its own as a dark & roomy bar/danceclub/lounge, with a great revolving series of dance parties and DJ nites. The weekend crowds have gotten large, but during the week happy hour is 5-9pm, with $2 Coronas & margaritas or $4 Absolut cosmos, otherwise known as the good stuff.

Voodoo Lounge & **Yo's Sushi Club** (2937 Mission St. at 25th, 285-3369, www.voodoolounge-sf.com; Yo's Sushi Club, 695-1799) is a bar, nightclub, and full sushi bar in one. If you want to do it all in one place, the Voodoo Lounge is your stop. The Voodoo also hosts live bands and weekly dance nites (call or check their website for listings). The best place to come for that last Mission Street nitecap and a hot bowl of miso soup. Strangely winning combination: Rum & coke and unagi maki.

SHOP STOPS

More than two words, **Cole Hardware** (3312 Mission at 29th, 647-8700, also the original at 956 Cole) is a way of life. Cole Hardware is the hardware family you always wanted; a jam-packed, super friendly, always knowledgeably staffed store with something for everyone, trust me. There's a Cole Hardware club card and a great regular newsletter. We've found everything from herb plants, fire screens, trash cans, lollipops, paints, garden hoses, wall clocks, and the ever necessary, plastic hooks. What Cole means by hardware is simply anything that will fit in the store, and then some. And bless them for it.

Big Lots! (Formerly MacFrugal's, for anyone keeping track, 3333 Mission, 648-5256) With the thick odor of cheap goods and junk in the air (don't let that scare you) and a bargain around every corner, this truly general store can quickly become an addiction. Six rolls of toilet paper (perfectly fine): 99 cents. Faux leopard slippery slippers: $2.99. Quite lovely ochre colored salad plates : 79 cents each. The fact that you NEVER know what you'll find is what really keeps us coming back for more (and more and more). At last, everything you never knew you needed under one roof. Free parking.

It turns out, even pets need manicures or 'pet'icures. So when playtime turns to bloodletting, we know it's time for our cat, Boo, to get her nails trimmed. **Bernie's Pet Supplies & Grooming** (1367 Valencia St. at 25th, 550-2323) offers nail trimming ($12) as well as general pet laundering (prices vary with pet size), and more importantly, it's a homey, full service neighborhood pet store with a great selection of food and pet toys. Boo's toy recommendation: catnip seahorse.

Tourists with disposable cameras will not mob you. You will not have to search for a parking place for an hour and a half. You will not be sucked into an enormous retail chain and sapped of all your cash. Potrero Hill is not a destination point. It's a real San Francisco neighborhood. Spend a day on the hill and you'll know why so many people move to San Francisco and never leave.

FIRST THINGS FIRST

Coffee. **Farley's** (1315 18th St. at Texas St., 648-1545). On Potrero Hill, these words are synonymous. For $1 plus tax, you are entitled to a large cup of Farley's brew and one refill. (If you drink more than that at a single sitting you should know that the bathroom is upstairs in the back.) Myriad sweets and treats crowd the counter, including great banana bread or toasted English muffins made to order. While you are drinking your cup o'joe, Farley's offers a number of satisfying diversions. Nearly 70 volumes of journals containing the joys and heartbreaks of Farley's customers over the last 8 years can keep your rapt for hours. If you're looking for something more objective, you'll be happy to find a selection of well over a hundred different current magazine titles on subjects from fashion to motorcross to keep you occupied. If you can't concentrate on the written word, you will soon notice that Farley's is a keen spot to watch people. You could even spy your future-ex.

BREAKFAST OF CHAMPIONS

Wheaties are for wussies. A real champion of San Francisco nightlife will not settle for a bowl of soggy wheat flakes in the morning. You need a strong antidote to the furies that have risen from the ashes of last night's pleasure. **Just for You** (1453 18th St. at Missouri St., 647-3033) might seat 20 people, tops. For as small as it is, they serve up a damn tasty, champion-sized breakfast. They've got everything from hotcakes to crab cakes, not to mention some mighty fine grits. If you go on a weekend, you won't be disappointed. Behind the counter you'll find movie star/director Tim Robbins deftly rancheroing your huevos and hashing your browns. (OK, it's not really Tim Robbins, his real name is Jarvis, but ooh, man, the resemblance is, you know, like, spooky.) And by the way, cell phones are verboten at Just for You. Turn it off, or you will be eating Wheaties for breakfast.

PLAYING HOOKY

Need to take a mental health day from work? Call and make an appointment for the tour at **Anchor Brewing**

Company (1705 Mariposa St. at Deharo, 863-8350). This medicine will cure what ails you. After the tour, they treat you to a tasting of their various brews and then you are invited to hang out and enjoy those brews at length in their private bar. If all goes well, you'll have to take another day off to recover.

EATS

It is purported that San Francisco has the highest number of restaurants per capita in the country. If Potrero Hill is any indication, this must be true. On the corner of 18th and Connecticut there are four restaurants, one on each corner. You can get almost anything you want on this corner. You have your California cuisine at **North Star Restaurant & Bakery** (288 Connecticut St. at 18th St., 551-9840). Casual service and a warmly lit interior make this intimate space good for a first date.

Aperto (1434 18th St. at Connecticut, 252-1625) has great Italian and really friendly service. It's the perfect place to take parents or to go to catch up with a friend you haven't seen in a while. Tanya & Salee used to take up two storefronts on the SE corner of the intersection, but now the restaurant has been made smaller and the **Lilo Lounge** (1469 18th St.) is in the corner spot. The two are still connected, so you can get appetizers from the restaurant while you sip tropical drinks in the tiki bar. **Goat Hill Pizza** (300 Connecticut St. at 18th, 641-1440) is a long-standing Potrero Hill landmark. Be sure to stop here on Monday nights, when you can get all-you-can-eat pizza and salad for a mere $8.50.

Just a half a block up on 18th St. is **Eliza's** (1457 18th St., at Connecticut, 648-9999), which is arguably the best Chinese food in the city. Locals swear by it. It's also a great place to go for lunch if you're on a budget, for about 5 bucks you get soup, tea, rice and the main dish of your choice.

DRINKING, ETC.

Sadie's Flying Elephant (491 Potrero Ave., 551-7988) is the place to go when you're feeling like a professional (a professional drinker, that is). It's a superdive with all the right ingredients; second hand furniture that is hardly suitable for a college student's fleabag apartment; two pool tables, and many drunken sharp shooters to play against; a dart board; a room with chalkboard walls, on which you are free to write in colored chalk that is provided by the establishment; a good jukebox; popcorn; strong, strong drinks; and a patronage that will not remember your embarrassing antics any more than you will.

If you're looking to break your secret Monday night sitcom habit or you're coming down off of a San Francisco Board of Tourism weekend at Fisherman's Wharf and Alcatraz, you can't beat **Blooms** (1318 18th St. at Texas St., 861-9467). Grab a couple friends, get some all-you can-eat grub at Goat Hill Pizza, and then head up to Blooms for a night of fun and excitement. Once you're suitably buzzed, take your beer and your friends to the back and enjoy a terrific view of the city skyline.

Follow the blue light and you'll end up at the bottom — the **Bottom of the Hill** (1233 17th St. at Missouri St., 621-4455). Don't expect to be able to have a tete-a-tete with your buddies. Do expect to hear some of the best new music that you can find anywhere in the city. On Sundays you can get all-you-can-eat barbecue accompanied by three bands for a modest cover.

SAN FRANCISCO AT NIGHT

All over the hill there are kick-ass views in every direction, and you don't have to squeeze yourself past 3 busloads of Midwestern tourists to see them. Nighttime is the right time for seeing the city from Potrero Hill. The location with one of the greatest views of San Francisco you'll ever see:

Corner of **18th and Kansas** and **20th and Minnesota** (everything from USF to the west, the skyline of downtown straight in front of you, and Oakland across the bay to the east), **18th St. overpass** above 280 (great city skyline).

OTHER STUFF ON POTRERO HILL

You've heard that Lombard St. is the curviest street in San Francisco. That isn't necessarily true. **Vermont St.** (at 20th St.) will certainly test your car's performance and your own reflexes. Added Bonus: no line of gawking tourists. If you need to send a souvenir to your sister's kid, go to the **Basic Brown Bear Factory** (444 DeHaro St. at Mariposa, 626-0781) where you can make your own personalized teddy bear and ship it off without much hassle. If you want to see some interesting art, but don't want to fight the gallery crowds, check out the walls and gallery at the newly remodeled **California College of Arts and Crafts** (1111 8th St., 16th St. at Wisconsin; 703-9500) at the foot of Potrero Hill, or if you are more classically inclined, go see the icons at **St. Gregory's Episcopal Church** (500 DeHaro St. at Mariposa, 255-1552).

DOGPATCH

The flatlands of Potrero Hill near the bay has a couple of clubs: **Pound SF** (Pier 96, 826-9202), an all-ages rock joint featuring bands like Death in June and Penis Flytrap. **Cafe Cocomo** (650 Indiana, 824-6810) is a DJ dance club 7 nights a week, no t-shirts, no jeans.

There's also a few bars, including the **Dogpatch Saloon** (2496 3rd St., 643-8592), and a tattoo/piercing parlor, **Dungeon** (2500 3rd St., 647-8644).

SOUTH OF MARKET
BY OLU JOHNSON

South of Market, or SoMa, is all about unexpected contrasts, both within the neighborhood and those cast against the rest of the city. A few blocks from the Museum of Modern Art (MoMa, 151 3rd St. at Mission, 357-4000) the overwhelming selection of leather chaps and corsets is yours to choose from, as well as that perfect X-rated cake that you have been searching for. This mix of high, low, and bizarre culture is merely the beginning. SoMa can seem remote and desolate until your eyes are trained. The buildings seamlessly glide into one another making it difficult to distinguish between a homeless shelter, an artist's loft, or a dot-com office space. Hidden housing is tucked away in surprisingly quiet charming alleys. SoMa is also very centrally located, with great access to all forms of public transportation on Market and Mission streets, including Muni, Muni underground, and Bart. All-night types appreciate a number of Owl (all night) bus lines, like the 14 Mission, N Judah, L Taraval, 5 Fulton, and 22 Fillmore (which passes through en route to Potrero).

A whole day could be spent visiting the shells of once proud companies like Petopia, Pets.com, Productopia, and the many other now-defunct dot-coms that altered SoMa. But if you're not feeling extremely morbid, then **Yerba Buena Gardens** and **Center for the Arts** (701 Mission at 3rd St., 978-2787) is another way to go. The lush grounds offer a convenient downtown spot to reflect in before going to the MoMA, plus you can mock all the shoppers filing in and out of the **Metreon**. You could spend time at the Metreon, but it's no different and more expensive than dozens of other malls. The Center hosts theater, dance, and music performances as well as film screenings; it also has a gallery - call to find out what's currently being featured. On the Northwest side of Mission is the **Cartoon Art Museum** (655 Mission at 3rd St., CAR-TOON, www.cartoonart.org) with exhibits featuring works by famous comic book artists and cartoonists, including Robert Crumb and Peanuts creator Charles Schulz. On the other side of the Center is an old-fashioned carousel, located next to **Zeum** (221 4th St. at Howard, 777-2800), the arts and technology museum designed primarily for kids ages 8-18 but there is something there for everyone. Some its best features are the multimedia rooms that let you design using the latest in video and computer design, and the artists space. Further down Fourth Street (the actual entrance is on 3rd) is the **Yerba Buena Ice Skating Center** (750 Folsom at 3rd St., 777-3727) if you like to skate year round, this is the spot; they also have hockey leagues for all you displaced east coasters missing your sports.

Another place to hang out during the day, and see some cool art featuring local artists is the **Minna Street Gallery**

(111 Minna St. at 2nd St., 974-1719) located in between Mission and Howard. They have a bar and at night the space transforms into a club featuring hot DJs and a lively scene. The atmosphere is a lot less stuck-up than some of the more austere galleries, and the art is usually better. There are some other art venues in SoMa (besides the MoMA), which offer a variety of events throughout the year. One of these, **New Langton Arts** (1246 Folsom at 8th St., 626-5416) was founded by a collection of San Francisco artists. It offers an exciting mix of visual and media arts, with music, performance, and literature also included. Another one, **Refusalon** (20 Hawthorne St., 546-0158), is a gallery space showing both national and international artists. They focus on experimental and conceptual art, and feature some of San Francisco's best artists. **SF Camerawork** (1246 Folsom at 8th St., 863-1001) obviously focuses on photography and art related to that medium. Another photo gallery that permanently features the work of a local great, is the **Ansel Adams Center** (655 Mission Street at 3rd St., 495-0318).

For some stellar local theater, usually highlighting women or local playwrights, try **Venue 9** (252 9th Street). It is a very nice space and I guarantee you'll never see one of those bad plays we all wished they'd kept on Broadway.

If making art is as important to you as supporting it, the king of all craft stores, **General Bead**, (Minna at 7th St., 255-2323) is located in the alley off 7th street and could be the happiest store in San Francisco. They have two floors of jewelry making implements and the staff is decorated in Day-Glo colors usually of their own creations. There is always something funky playing on the stereo and you can tell that they are having a good time. **Pearl Arts and Crafts** (969 Market, 357-1400) is another art store and the young knowledgeable staff can help you with all of your art needs. If you go to Pearl be sure to check out the paper section upstairs because the materials and designs will certainly inspire you.

Another off beat spot that I would recommend is the **flower mart** near the Bay Bridge (6th at Harrison) featuring the fake flower mart. There are also plenty of real flowers as well for all of your urban garden needs. Finally, no trip through SoMa should neglect the **Defenestration building** located at the corner of 6th and Howard. The building has an assortment of objects like sofas, TVs, and lamps, seemingly frozen in the act of being thrown out the window.

After wondering why every city doesn't have a building with furniture in motion, you might be hungry and SoMa is full of good grub that doesn't take a large bite out of your budget. San Francisco is home of the burrito, and few places in the city are better than **El Balazo** (5th St. at Mission) the vegetarian and specialty burritos are filled with unusual but good fillings, like zucchini, and cactus. Their pork tacos are especially good and the tamales are handmade. The key to any burrito though is good Spanish rice, and theirs is excellent. **AK Subs** (8th St. at Harrison, 241-9600) is a perennial favorite and almost its entire menu is under five dollars. Another cheap spot that has been feeding the SoMa crowd is **Bill's Kitchen** (475 3rd St. at Bryant 541-0699). Bill's menu consists mainly of tasty burgers and lunch fare and is, like AK Subs, extremely cheap and good. Thai food restaurants are ubiquitous in San Francisco and SoMa has two good ones that are located very close to one another and neither one will leave your wallet empty. **Manora's** (1600 Folsom at 12th St., 861-6224) right across the street from **Harvey's SoMa Burgers** (1582 Folsom, 626-1985), has excellent curries and **Just Thai** (1532 Howard at 10th St., 431-3113) has extensive vegetarian choices. For something a little different try **Tu Lan** (6th at Market, 626-0927). I've eaten almost the entire menu and have not been disappointed at all. Don't be dissuaded by the linoleum floors or fluorescent lighting, the food is perennially recognized as among the best Vietnamese at any price in the city. The only thing to be afraid of is eating too much because the food is almost addictive. Tu Lan is very cheap, and once you eat there, it will be easy to see how it can survive in its location. The interior of **Big Nate's** (12th at Folsom, 861-4242) is the reason that most of the business is delivery or take-out. It's very drab and reminiscent of eating in a school cafeteria. The food redeems it with the chicken, ribs, and brisket being spectacular, but then again, they could put that barbecue sauce on just about anything and I would eat it. The prices start at about $8 and combo meals start at $14. **India Garden** (9th at Folsom, 622-2798) has locations in other parts of the city, but the outdoor garden in this converted Victorian makes this the premier location. If you just want to grab a quick slice of pie during your day or refuel at night, **Chico's Pizza** (986 Mission at 6th St., 777-9909) is the place. They stay open late so you can grab a slice while clubbing through SoMa. Another pizza store is **Extreme Pizza** (1052 Folsom at 7th St., 701-9000). Their pizza isn't the greatest, but the subs and cheap beer prices might warrant a visit. For more late night food you could try **Mel's Drive-in** (801 Mission at 4th, 227-4477) located across from the Metreon. The food isn't great but it is open all night.

Other low cost options in SoMa are supermarkets such as **Trader Joe's** (555 9th St. at Bryant, 863-1292) and **Rainbow Grocery** (1745 Folsom at 13th St., 863-0621), an all-natural grocery store, bent towards the Whole Foods, vegan reality.

If you are looking to spend a little more money, or want to have a special night, there are plenty of other food options that range from merely fancy to extremely bizarre. If you would like a singular dining experience that could only be had in SoMa, check out **Asia SF** (201 9th St. at Folsom, 255-2742). They serve a fusion of Asian and Californian cuisine to a show put on by dancing drag queens. The performers, catwalk their way along the tabletops and are fabulously costumed and accessorized. It is a great place for parties, but it does get fairly loud. Another place for parties or if you are out with a large group and want a chance to be loud, is **Buca Di Beppo** (855 Howard at 5th St., 543-7673). This restaurant serves oversized portions of pasta family style. Each meatball alone must weigh close to two pounds. Around the corner is **Le Charm** (315 5th St. at Howard, 546-6128) a small French bistro that is very good but is definitely more on the expensive side. A little deeper in SoMa on the way to the stadium is a place that makes a great drink and serves food as well. **Infusion** (555 2nd St. at Harrison, 543-2282) is a tiny restaurant named for their many flavors of vodka infused with fruit. **Fly Trap** (606 Folsom at 2nd St., 243-0580) serves good California cuisine without being overly fancy. The result is that you have a chance to sample some four star cuisine at two star prices. All of the above dinner places will run between $10-15 an entrée, with the exception of Le Charm, but it's French food, so c'est la vie. There are so many more places, if the place you want to go has a wait, then walk around the block, there is bound to be something else appetizing near by.

If you want to go really upscale then SoMa has some of the best in the city as well. Located next to each other on Folsom are **Azie** and **Lulu** (826 Folsom at 4th St., 538-0918; 816 Folsom at 4th St., 495-5775), they are prohibitively expensive and it would be rude to mention how much a meal there would cost, but the food is good. **Chaya** (132 The Embarcadero, 777-8688) is located on the Embarcadero with great views of the bay, and even better sushi. On weekends all of these places are a little crowded though so you may want to consider making a reservation.

The cafés in SoMa are a little more limited, especially in contrast with the rest of the city. The good part is that they aren't as packed with self-proclaimed café professionals who know the exact way to hold that book of esoteric poetry, or the haughtiest way to furrow their brow. My favorite is **Caffé SoMa** (1601 Howard at 11th St., 861-5012). The scene is mellow and the jukebox is filled with Jazz and Blues at just 25 cents per song. Another one that I sometimes hit is **Tony Baloneys** (no joke! 1098 Howard at 9th St., 863-1514), but the owner is also a club promoter so they aren't always open when you think they should be. Walk by on a Sunday morning trying to stave off that empty-headed feeling with some coffee and you might find them closed. So you keep going to **Brainwash** (1122 Folsom at 7th St., 437-2363) where the service is slow, and the food is average and rather expensive. They do have live performances including comedy, spoken word, and bands. They are also a full service Laundromat so you may want to do a few loads of laundry since it may take that long to get your meal. Another café I would check out is the **Internet Café** (Market at 6th), which could have a different name by the time you read this. One of its main attractions is that it's close to the Warfield on Market Street with outdoor seating, so the people watching is terrific.

The bars and clubs are really the heart of SoMa and they are no less varied than anything else that it has to offer. One of my favorites is **POW!** (101 6th St. at Mission, 278-0940). The interior is walled with Anime style paintings, and their motto is "Be a superhero, or just drink like one." They feature Ultra Hour, which lasts from 4-8 p.m., and on any given night some of the city's hottest DJs are spinning records. When you go to POW! ask for a Chocolate Cake or one of their specialty cocktails. During the week check out **El Bobo** (1539 Folsom at 11th St., 861-6822). It has a neighborhood bar feel to it but the food is not your standard bar-fare. The menu rotates depending on the season but one fixture is the Guinness chocolate cake. It is definitely a chill spot, and one that you go to on weekends when you don't feel like hanging from a rack in a meat market. For more happy hours in a bar with a comfortable feel, try **Cassidy's** (1145 Folsom at 7th St., 241-9990). They usually have a daily special, and are conveniently located near all the hostels on Folsom Street. Plus it has televisions so if you want, you can watch the San Francisco Giants. A lot of the bike messengers hang out here so the atmosphere is distinctly SoMa and unpretentious. **The Tempest** (431 Natoma, 495-1863) recently reopened after changing ownership and has emerged as a place to hear live bands. On some nights it's a little dead, and then you may want to go around the corner to the **Hotel Utah** (500 4th St. at Bryant, 546-6300). The bartenders are friendly and the crowd is eclectic, and the ribs are good. For a little more straightforward action there is the **Glas Kat** (520 4th St. at Bryant, 495-6626) where the crowd tends to be a little GAP but sometimes the music is good. One San Francisco institution that must mentioned, is **The Stud** (339 9th. St. at Harrison, 252-7883) that has been an intricate part of the gay scene since the '70s. The crowd is always full of energy and they feature special nights like Freak Show, which lives up to its billing. The bar welcomes everyone, except for maybe the straight and narrow.

A lot of the bars just mentioned do have DJs spinning all the hot grooves, but if you want to dance all night there are a few places that keep rocking until four or beyond. Every night of the week there is always a party at **Ten15 Folsom** (1015 Folsom St., 431-1200) that contains a many dance floors on three levels all rocking different genres of music.

It is a big club and can be overwhelming, so if you want a smaller, tighter party try **Cat Club** (1190 Folsom at 8th St., 431-3332). They have different theme parties; like rock nights featuring music like Bowie, to New Wave retro nights with music like Siouxie and the Banshees or the Cure. The **DNA Lounge** (375 11th St. at Harrison, 626-1409) recently reopened with a state of the art light and sound system. The new owner created Netscape and I guarantee this club is better than his browser. Another spot is **Rawhide II** (280 7th St. at Howard, 621-1197), which began originally as a place for gays and lesbians to listen to country music. It has been transformed through time and the dominance of DJ culture into a dance club. Although unlike most clubs in this city, at Rawhide II you can hear both old and new hip-hop.

If it's 4 a.m., and it looks like you're going to be up all night, and you still need to feel the deep thump of the bass in your chest, and your feet have to keep moving, head down to Folsom to the **End Up** (401 6th St. at Harrison, 357-0827). The alcohol stops at 2, but the party keeps going until the sun comes up. At 6 they restart serving so if you need to, you can drink again. There are also larger European styled dance clubs that fit a few hundred party-goers near the ones mentioned above. They are loud though so if it sounds good, take the plunge. The cover charges at those places tend to be high, $15 or more, so don't be surprised.

SoMa has plenty of places to see really good rock or other types of performances. On Market Street itself there is the **Warfield** (982 Market at 6th St., 775-7722), which has a variety of acts. Everyone from Top 40 Pop bands to Greg Allman and friends might play there. The venue is large with balcony seating and tight security that will under no circumstances let you create a fire hazard. Another SoMa venue that focuses on smaller indie label talent is **Slim's** (333 11th St. at Harrison, 255-0333). The place is small so it's really easy to get into the music. Some of the best shows I've ever seen in San Francisco were at Slims.

With the all the fanfare about SoMa, I'm sure you are waiting for the other shoe to drop, well here it comes. Although San Francisco is a very safe city as far as urban metropolises go, if there is anything resembling a skid row, it exists on either side of Market between 6th and 7th Streets. A dense concentration of SRO hotels and the influence of the Tenderloin only a few blocks north adds to the mix. A few of the places listed above fall within this area, but the safety threat is definitely more perceived than actual. The key is to handle yourself well and pay attention to your surroundings - especially when you're leaving clubs buzzed. People may spare change you, but you don't have to give it to them. You also don't have to be rude.

One unlikely highlight of this area occurs on **Stevenson Alley**. From 7th all the way to 5th Street, this is a virtual Hooverville, and is the skungiest alley not in a third world country. It is also home to one of the best murals in San Francisco. There is also a pedestrian bridge linking two buildings that looks absolutely stunning in the sunset. The other unintended bonus about the neighborhood is that parking is more available here than anywhere else. There are a few lots scattered about, and there's tons of street parking on Folsom, Howard, and the numbered cross streets. As you drive through people will hail you into spots, but do not feel pressured to give them money for things they don't own. Overall, I would say that the safety of your material possessions is in far more risk than any personal harm; with any harm at all being very unlikely. A good tip is to not leave items of any value visible in a parked car. In fact because of the way the area is perceived, a lot of artists live in and around SoMa, which is what adds an extra bit of character to the locals you may encounter.

**HAIGHTIN' IT
BY LORI NOLL**

Just like real San Franciscans never call the city "Frisco," they don't call this neighborhood "Haight Ashbury," as the rest of the world does. Actually, that particular corner, with its irksome Gap and popular Ben and Jerry's ice cream shop is not the pride and joy of those who lovingly call the Haight home. But it is entertaining to watch the tourists in faux tie-dye taking pictures with the street sign.

My two favorite things to do in this district are peoplewatch and eat. A lot of the little restaurants along the street have great window seats, so you can do both at the same time. **The Pork Store Cafe** (1451 Haight at Ashbury, 864-6981) is perfect for this pastime. They have huge portions for reasonable prices. Get there earlyish because they close at 3 p.m., and avoid brunch hours on weekends: the line gets all the way up the block. Order an omelet and grits and stare out the window guessing which bums are really rich kids ditching a day at private school. Breakfast is also good and cheap at **All You Knead** (1466 Haight at Ashbury, 552-4550), and you can sit there drinking coffee forever without a waitress lurking, anxious to turn your table over. I've never eaten there but I hear **Kate's Kitchen** (471 Haight at Fillmore, 626-3984) in the Lower Haight is tasty, too.

For burritos, it's a toss up between **El Balazo** (1654 Haight St. at Clayton, 864-8608) and the fiesta-like **Zona Rosa** (1797 Haight at Shrader, 668-7717). **Chebella's** (1801 Haight St. at Masonic, 751-6204) has yummy nachos but just a warning, this place isn't nicknamed "Che' Belly Ache" for nothing. The truth is if you really want authentic Mexican food, head to the Mission.

Haight has pretty good pizza by the slice too. I like thin, crispy crust which is best at **Escape from New York** (1737 Haight St. at Cole, 668-5577). I get cheese and mushroom, but the brave swear by their signature "You say Potato," which has pesto sauce, sautéed potatoes and whole cloves of roasted garlic. This is not date food. For fans of thick crust, go to **Fat Slice** (1535 Haight St. at Clayton, 552-4200). Sandwiches and salads are fresh at **People's Cafe** (1419 Haight St. at Masonic, 553-8842), as are the tasty cilantro and noodles at **Citrus Club** (1790 Haight at Cole, 387-6366).

When you find yourself with a large group of loud friends, head to either **Cha Cha Cha** (1801 Haight St. at Shrader, 386-5758) or **Kan Zaman** (1793 Haight St. at Shrader, 751-9656). Cha Cha Cha is a trendy Caribbean restaurant that's bursting with colorful 3D decorations, like bullfighting scenes and Virgin Mary shrines. They serve tapas, so you order little dishes like fried calamari and platanos with beans and share them. Always order sangria at about the ratio of a quarter-pitcher to every person at least. Kan Zaman is a Middle Eastern restaurant that doubles as a hookah bar. The flavored tobacco changes daily, spanning from apricot to vanilla. Both places are on the more expensive side, but still a good place to meet friends for dinner on payday.

It's safe to say that Haight is a fun spot to windowshop, and generally a not-so-ideal place to buy things. Stores like **Villains** (1653 Haight at Belvedere, 864-7727) and **Ambiance** (1458 Haight St. at Masonic, 552-5095) have cool clothes, but are crazily overpriced, at least for those of us who like to have money left over to eat after we dress ourselves. The secondhand or "thrift" stores like **Buffalo Exchange** (1555 Haight at Clayton, 431-7733), **Wasteland** (1660 Haight St. at Clayton, 863-3150) and **Held Over** (1543 Haight St. at Ashbury, 864-0818) aren't so thrifty either, but if you have a lot of time to browse or some imaginative fashion sense, you can find good deals on vintage clothes at these spots. And if your old clothes are hip enough by their standards, they'll trade with you or give you a little cash for them.

Haight is the holy land for hard-to find-footwear though. **Shoe Biz I**, **II**, and **III** (1446, 1553 Haight Street at Clayton, 864-0990; 861-3933) sell casual, sporty and dressy shoes respectively. I have to admit the treasures found here are overpriced, but alas, shoes are my weakness so it's hard to be objective. I don't find it unreasonable to sell my soul for a pair of modish shoes from **John Fluvog** (1697 Haight at Cole, 436-9784), where a sign wishes "Peace, good sole and groovy love vibe to those who enter." If you're into it, you can find fetish shoes at **DalJeets** (1773 Haight St. at Shrader, 668-8500) where they specialize in anything silver-studded. They also have extra large sizes for the stiletto-wearing man in your life.

If the exquisite peoplewatching and the signs reading "Don't you even think about peeing here" posted on resident garages are not entertainment enough, head to the independent **Red Vic Movie House** (1727 Haight at Shrader, 668-3994) to catch a flick. Admission is reasonable; $4.50 for the 2 p.m. showing and $6.50 in the evenings. Or lose yourself in the stacks of dusty books at **Forever After Books** (1475 Haight at Ashbury, 431-8299) or the anarchist bookstore, **Bound Together** (1369 Haight at Masonic, 431-8355). **Happy Trails** (1615 Haight, 431-7232) has retro kitsch and fun stuff galore. The magazine section at **Anubis Warpus** (1525 Haight at Ashbury, 431-2218) is impressive, but if you want to get pierced or tattooed, the rumor is that **Cold Steel** (1783 Haight at Cole, 933-7233) is cleaner. Rent skates for $6 an hour, even the old-fashioned kind with wheels on four corners at **Skates on Haight** (1818 Haight at Stanyan, 752-8375).

If you're going to live around here, you have to learn to save some change on everyday activities. Get hip haircuts for cheap at **Bladerunners** (1792 Haight at Shrader, 751-1723) on Monday or Wednesday afternoons by volunteering to be a hair model. 'Do's are only $15, a fraction of the $55 and up cuts they usually offer. Call for an appointment. Forgo the gym membership and go to **Hoy's Sports** (1632 Haight at Clayton, 252-5370) instead. The staff preaches everything known to man about feet. Invest in a good pair of running shoes and go for a jog around the track in the Panhandle. For a better workout, try the hilly but beautiful **Buena Vista Park**, off of Haight Street between upper and lower Haight. At the end of the stretch, **Cala Foods** (Haight at Stanyan, 752-3940) is not the best grocery store in town but it's open 24 hours and has parking.

At night, **The Top** (424 Haight, 864-7386) on lower Haight has good music, the drinks are strong, and as the

Bay Guardian says, "the people there are more interested in dancing than in watching how badly you dance." **Nickie's Barbecue** (460 Haight at Fillmore, 621-6508) also in the lower Haight, is also a swell place to dance with friends. **Hobson's Choice** (1601 Haight St. at Clayton, 621-5859) has $2 drink specials during happy hour and boasts 100 different kinds of rum. The place is packed at night and from the looks of it the people are interesting, if not interesting to gawk at. **Persian aub Zam Zam** (1633 Haight at Belvedere, 861-2545) has famous martinis.

For odds and ends, there are plenty of smoke shops, and a drawing of a half-naked girl riding the shaft of a pipe claims that **Pipe Dreams** (1376 Haight at Masonic, 431-3553) is the oldest smoke shop in the city, which sounds good to me. For coffee, pool, piano and internet access all in one place, **Rockin' Java** (1821 Haight at Stanyan, 831-8842) is the place to frequent, if you can stand the ancient furniture and unidentifiable smell. Out-of-towners and locals alike are in awe of **Amoeba Music** (1855 Haight at Stanyan, 831-1200), which is a huge warehouse of music bargains. Snag obscure vinyl at **Recycled Records** (1377 Haight at Masonic, 626-4075), liquid body latex at **Bal La Riga Leather** (1391 Haight St. at Masonic, 552-1525) and a denser, more enjoyable bagel at **Manhattan Bagel** (1206 Masonic at Haight, 626-9111). On the streets, look for an artist named Joseph Clark who has been arrested 7 times on Haight Street for displaying his art. He has no store, no business cards, and claims to have art on all continents but Antarctica. His abstract pieces aren't bad either, but if you're not interested in art, he can direct you to a good place to eat.

Finally, don't walk around Haight or the Panhandle alone after dark, don't buy drugs from folks off the street, and don't be seduced into buying crap you don't need by sexy window dressing.

HISTORICAL HAIGHT ASHBURY

Besides being one of the peoplewatching capitols of the world, the Haight Ashbury is steeped in rock n'roll history.

112 Lyon: Janis Joplin's house.

142 Central: Jimi Hendrix lived here.

710 Ashbury: The Grateful Dead house.

130 Delmar: Where the Jefferson Airplane lived before fame and fortune bought them a mansion at 2400 Fulton.

636 Cole: House of Manson (where Charlie, Squeaky, and the rest of the gang lived before heading south to LA).

318 Parnassus: Gonzo journalist Hunter S. Thompson lived here while writing *Hell's Angels*.

2500 block of Geary: Richard Brautigan lived here in the '60s, before he moved north to Bolinas.

Courtney Love used to live in the lower Haight and rumor has it that a few years ago after a Hole show at the Fillmore Auditorium, she jumped on a 22-Fillmore bus and inebriatedly announced as the bus crossed Hayes Street, "I used to live right there!"

NORTH BEACH AND CHINATOWN BY V. VALE

During the Beat Era in San Francisco ('50s - early '60s), there was a decrepit peeling-paint bar in North Beach called The Place where my father - one of the only Asian beatniks in "the Scene" - used to hang out. Now it's a graphic design studio. That, in a nutshell, gives a quick snapshot of how North Beach has changed in the past half-century (and in this writer's opinion, not for the better). But some would say that it all depends on what your values are, or your point of view. If your values don't exalt poetry, art, philosophy and literature, you probably aren't reading this anyway. We must content ourselves with ever-diminishing expectations and appreciate the little that's left of San Francisco's North Beach bohemian legacy. At least we still have **Bimbo's 365 Club**, one of the most beautiful (and perfectly preserved and maintained) art-deco/'50s-decor 800-capacity nightclubs left in the city of Saint Francis, (1030 Columbus at Chestnut, 474-0365). A visit to this club is highly recommended, and do not miss the naked "mermaid" in the fishbowl at the main bar. The enchanting paintings and statuary scattered throughout are possible to overlook if one's focus is on the entertainment stage - everyone from Sam Butera to 8-1/2 Souvenirs to retro showbiz acts such as SuperDiamond (an homage to Neil, of course). Bimbo's has never shed its elegance or courtliness, even during the scruffy '60s - that's because it has remained family-owned and operated and has never been corporate.

Light supper jazz can occasionally be heard at **Enrico's** (504 Broadway at Kearny, 982-6223), the basement of the **Black Cat** (501 Broadway at Kearny St., 981-2233), **Rose Pistola** (532 Columbus at Green St., 399-0499), **Moose's** (1652 Stockton at Filbert, 989-7800), and a tiny bar on Grant Ave next to the Nature Stop.

Louder, more raucous blues/rock/rockabilly can be heard at **The Saloon** (1232 Grant at Columbus, 989-7666), San Francisco's oldest bar, and the **Grant/Green** bar, where local legend Johnny Nitro often presides ("She's got one foot in the East/One foot in the West/Johnny Nitro in the middle/Doing what he does best"). The aforementioned Saloon often features ex-luminaries from bands like Country Joe and the Fish, Quicksilver Messenger Service, the Paul Butterfield Blues Band as well as rockabilly stalwarts the Bachelors (a personal favorite).

Anyone undertaking a walking tour of San Francisco could do worse than to stroll leisurely up Grant Avenue, starting at downtown San Francisco and threading one's way through Chinatown toward North Beach, which is bordered roughly by Broadway and Columbus to Bay and Sansome. First on the list of recommended visits is **City Lights**

Bookstore (261 Columbus at Broadway, 362-1901) founded by beat poet Lawrence Ferlinghetti and Peter Martin (long-departed) in the mid-'50s, and long a battleground for freedom of speech and avant-garde cultural and political thought. Once busted for selling (and publishing) the seminal Allen Ginsberg poetry book, *Howl*, City Lights has consistently fought censorship and conservatism trends, and stayed up-to-the-minute. North Beach is also blessed with two outstanding used bookstores, **Black Oak Books** (540 Broadway at Romolo, 986-3872) down from the **RE/Search publications** office (20 Romolo #B, 362-1465) and **Carroll's Books** (633 Vallejo at Columbus, 397-6364). **Broadway Cigars & Liquors** (550 Broadway at Columbus, 397-1310) a.k.a. the Dirty Bookstore provides a large periodical/newspaper selection. Scattered throughout Chinatown are a number of mostly Chinese-language only book/magazine stores. Lastly, there is a bookstore featuring only travel books at Jackson at Columbus.

As North Beach and San Francisco have become overrun with high-priced yuppie eateries (the most restaurants per capita in the U.S.), resident ethnic cuisine conservators yet make it possible for locals (and savvy visitors) to dine deliciously - even enthusiastically - at affordable prices. After a few hours perusing the hard-to-find independent and university press titles at City Lights Bookstore (the very opposite of a chain store), one might feel the urgent need for an appetizing and life-enhancing repast at the humble **Vietnamese My Canh** (626 Broadway at Columbus, 397-8888), run by three generations of an extended friendly family. Open from 11 a.m. until 2 or 3 in the morning to serve a loyal and mostly Asian local clientele, this restaurant has a wide variety of offerings for both vegetarians and carnivores, and upon request will make dishes not listed on the extensive menu. On a recent visit one of my friends ordered Kung Pao shrimp with vegetables - not on the menu - and it was hot, savory and exhilarating. Because of its extensive patronage (On-the-Road Rule No. 1: Never eat at a deserted diner) the vegetables, tofu, etc. are always fresh. In a decade of dining - probably literally a thousand meals - never have I nor my companions suffered gastric distress. And so far, there's never been a wait.

On Kearny between Pacific and Jackson stands the deservedly-famous (written up in 1001 guidebooks) **House of Nanking** (919 Kearny, 421-1429) featuring the pioneering cuisine of Peter Fang and his wife, émigrés from the province of Nanking. Almost singlehandedly they introduced yams/sweet potatoes into the niche victuals known as "Chinese food." Proud of the fact that they use nothing canned (although I once saw them bring a dollyful of 50-lb sugar sacks into the premises, and my wife spotted industrial-size containers of Skippy peanut butter), uberchef Peter often says, "Trust me," and brings out dish after dish of wondrously varied vegetables, seafood, chicken and beef. As an excessively-regular patron I was often treated to free mini-servings from the Fangs' own meals (usually prepared about 2:30 in the afternoon) and one particularly memorable dish featured cabbage in sesame oil prepared with fresh Bing cherry slices. It's amazing how rapidly their cooks can prepare multi-course meals in a small kitchen reminiscent of Tokyo efficiency-hotel rooms. Noteworthy: servings are generous (I always take home leftovers), everything is spotlessly clean, and at night the ultra-bustling atmosphere reminds one of the marketplace featured in *Blade Runner*. When you eat at the Nanking you feel alive. It's actually worth the wait in line, but I always go between 2-4:45 p.m.

One of the best-kept local secrets is **Chef Jia's** (925 Kearny at Jackson, 398-1626), right next to the House of Nanking but rarely as crowded (so far). Perhaps taking a cue from their famous neighbor, the chef not only began integrating yams/sweet potatoes into his cuisine but has since outdone himself preparing a plethora of dishes not found anywhere else: Mandarin orange prawns, spicy yams, and my personal favorite: the sizzling bean curd iron platter (which usually includes yams, broccoli, zucchini, mushrooms, string beans and more - a complete meal for the itinerant vegetarian).

There are hundreds more restaurants within ten square blocks of City Lights, and undoubtedly most of them offer adequate-to-exceptional fare. For example, **Golden Flower** (667 Jackson at Grant, 433-6469) serves excellent Vietnamese soups (although I always leave feeling a little hungry); **Yuet Lee** (1300 Stockton at Broadway, 982-6020) open til 3 a.m., has consistently delicious seafood and unique vegetable dishes in great sauces, although I wish their servings were 20% larger; **Sam Woh's** (813 Washington at Grant, 982-0596) has had an unparalleled downscale atmosphere for decades (the legendary, insulting/friendly waiter Edsel Ford Fong died a few years back) and delicious rice soups.

There are many bakeries offering cheap treats and snacks (an outstanding bakery on Grant Avenue near Jackson St. even has wheat bread offerings, and always has a line). For cheap Italian food it's still hard to beat the now-mini-chain **Pasta Pomodoro** (1875 Union at Columbus, 771-7900) They always have a $7 lunch special of pasta, salad and bread and they're perennially crowded (deservedly so). But my favorite "deal" is the weekday $5.95 lunch at **Viva** (1224 Grant at Columbus, 989-8482) with pasta-salad-garlic bread (much preferable to normal bread) offerings and choice of pesto, tomato or Bolognese (hamburger) sauce. I also prefer their pizza recipes to those of my previous favorite, North Beach Pizza - particularly since they evicted the

Prudente Deli from the neighborhood. For vegetarians, Viva has an amply well-rounded selection of pastas and salads (my friend Dishwasher Pete's favorite is the B-S-P: broccoli, spinach and pesto), my only complaint being that the red wine is served in a smallish water glass instead of a wine glass (but at least it's usually a robust vintage).

On the more upscale side, a favorite Italian eatery has remained: **L'Osteria** (519 Columbus at Union, 982-1124), run by two women who toughed out the challenge of opening a small undercapitalized restaurant and by delicious recipes quickly built up a loyal clientele. The place is tiny so expect to wait, but everything on the menu is absolutely delicious. Excellent choice for those on a diet. It's right across from superstar chef Reed Hearon's deservedly famous **Rose Pistola** (532 Columbus at Green, 399-0499) which is best enjoyed when relatives or better-off cohorts take you out to dinner. Rose Pistola often has decent light jazz music, too, without the annoying (but necessary - musicians gotta eat, too) obligation to fend off solicitations for contributions. The Ligurian cuisine offers plenty for the vegetarian; in fact a meal of vegetable courses can easily suffice... although they have a unique way with seafood... in fact, everything. Rose Pistola's quality control is superb, and sometimes they have a flaming dessert available which can help spark romantic ideas. This is a place for special occasions, and is often crowded; Monday or Tuesday nights or generally the 5 p.m. time slot is recommended for those who hate standing around and waiting.

One of the most traditional and soulful Italian eateries is **Tomasso's** (1042 Kearny at Broadway, 398-9696). With booths and a long center communal table, this restaurant is usually crowded. It's very good basic Italian cuisine in healthy-sized portions (always fresh) offer a mute reminder that the California culinary revolution, with its emphasis on rare ingredients (heirloom tomatoes, grapeseed oil, arugula - all of which *are* tantalizing) and astonishing combinations, may sometimes wax overwhelmingly precious... just give us some satisfying home-cooked food, fer chrissakes.

There are several Chinese vegetarian restaurants, the **Lucky Creation** (850 Washington at Grant, 989-0818), quite tiny but definitely good. Another favorite Chinese restaurant is the venerable **Far East Cafe** (631 Grant at Sacramento, 982-3245). It features private booths with buzzers, enormous Chinese lanterns that came around the horn. This is a beautifully preserved restaurant that deserves landmark status.

On Broadway near Columbus, the venerable semi-outdoor **Enrico's** café (504 Broadway at Kearny, 982-6223) still draws a healthy weekend crowd of gawkers who dine and enjoy the passing parade of humanity. Jazz groups such as Lavay Smith and Her Red-Hot Skillet Lickers and Mal Sharpe's Big Money in Jazz Band (both recommended) can be heard weekend nights. City Lights Bookstore has an account there to entertain itinerant book salesmen as well as visiting luminaries; just before he died in 1997, Allen Ginsberg took some photos of me and my baby daughter in her stroller there. The food is pricey but all right (neighboring competition is fierce in the exquisite cuisine department, what with Reed Hearon's **Black Cat** cafe across the street, which offers intriguing fusion dishes and has a basement cafe featuring jazz musicians and even occasional poetry readings). Enrico's used to be open til 3 a.m. every night; I interviewed bands such as the Screamers from Los Angeles during the late-'70s heyday of the early punk cultural revolution. In those days we could only afford coffee; our idea of eating out for nourishment was late-night **Clown Alley** (42 Columbus at Pacific Ave., 421-2540), and the more upscale **Golden Dragon** (816 Washington at Grant, 398-

3920) where one night shortly after I and a party of fellow punk rockers departed, young Chinese gangster-wannabes walked in and sprayed the joint with bullets, back in 1977. The resultant global publicity closed down the Chinatown late-night tourist trade forever... Grant Avenue instantly became a ghost town at night.

Chinatown offers everything anyone would ever need to survive, at the lowest possible prices: food, clothes, household necessities. There are several large spaces (with no English-language signage outside) offering unbelievably cheap odds-and-ends (everything from lamps to shoes to dishes to Tupperware to outdated Chinese *Penthouse* magazines). One such place occupies the former Woolworths (R.I.P., a chain which supplied me with dozens of cut-on LPs back in the pre-CD years, like the Mae West Rock'n'Roll album for 99 cents) on **Stockton near Vallejo** (across from Walgreen's). Come to think of it, this store is the Chinese inheritor of the Woolworths' legacy and offers almost as wide a variety of cheap merchandise - Chinatown "outlet" stores like this are the populist Woolworths of today. A slight drawback is a pervasive effluvium of strange mothball-like chemicals. But it offers great bargains for anyone seeking to furnish a room or apartment, or in search of cheap weird gifts for friends. The store is maximally jammed with merchandise and the aisles are so narrow one must navigate sideways, inevitably knocking something over.

Another favorite Chinese "everything-but-the-kitchen sink" outlet store is on the site of a former Chinatown movie theater (**Jackson at Stockton**), frequented in the '70s and '80s by punk rockers and other dissidents who appreciated the low prices and the opportunity to see films that were rarely (or never) listed in any "History of Cinema" books, even the relatively recent Hong Kong cinema books in English. The title of one particularly memorable film was translated as "Concentration Camp for Goils" [sic]; it was - you guessed it - a charmingly "ethnic" variant of the Women-in-Prison genre, featuring Asian women in U.S. army drag enacting various cruel and disciplinary scenarios. Too much! These days the cavernous space offers cheap children's clothes, all kinds of men's and women's clothing, low-price down comforters and cotton pajamas... whatever the market will bear.

It's right next to my favorite Chinese **produce stand**. Favorite because the two ladies who work there actually remember me, let me use their bathroom, give personal service and even special quantity discounts - as opposed to the many other gloriously cheap but briskly businesslike and impersonal produce markets in Chinatown. They're the only Chinese produce store to boast a fresh orange juice-making machine ($1 a cup).

Both tourists and locals occasionally take photos, and my favorite one-hour photo developing shop is **Photo Focus** (1100 Stockton at Jackson, 391-4745). This place not only maintains consistent quality control (chemicals are changed regularly) but gives you a free photo book and your next roll of film - usually Kodak Gold 100 ASA film. The owners are smart and friendly: recently they saved a roll of film that was stuck in my Olympus point-and-shoot when it died on a trip to Mexico City.

The friendly **Gong Num Camera Shop** (913 Grant at Washington, 982-4331) is run by the same Chinese lady with the '50s hairdo and glasses for the past 40 years, at least. She's sharp, articulate, bilingual and also carries (at this writing) the hard-to-find tiny DV videocassettes for the new generation of digital mini-video-cameras at reasonable prices.

Almost next door is a favorite Chinese **stationery** store (been there for years) where you can get cheap red hardbound notebooks from China, dozens of kinds of pens and pencils, and a variety of papers - in short, all manner of writing-related materials that are hard to find. Next door they have Chinese writing seals: impress your friends by stamping a red Chinese character for "love" on your next missive.

Shopping sometimes inspires thirst, and one of the most atmospheric out-of-the-past bars in Chinatown lingers nearby: the beautiful **Li Po** (916 Grant at Jackson, 982-0072). The Li Po has an enormous lantern and vintage decrepit standard bar interior with high barstools, but the place also has a lingering redolence of long-departed opium habituees and Chinese courtesans in silk dresses with thigh-high slits up the side. This is a good spot to avoid anyone you don't want to run into; it's small but oddly memorable - the kind of place you imagine Robert Mitchum might have frequented in the '50s.

Going east and further upscale is the **Café Niebaum-Coppola** (916 Kearny at Columbus, 291-1700) in the shadow of the gorgeous Francis Ford Coppola-owned triangular art-deco flatiron building at Pacific and Columbus, a landmark edifice of architectural splendor. Far more upscale than its predecessors, the cafe boasts Coppola's own vintages, upscale gourmet food and outdoor tables - although one is subject to liberal quantities of car exhaust emissions. But this is a place to hobnob with visiting film-world luminaries (Coppola and associates can often be seen discussing scripts, or whatever) and perhaps network with other Bay Area film workers.

Less ostentatious yet quietly power-broker-friendly is Jeanette Etheridge's acclaimed **Tosca** cafe (242 Columbus Ave. at Broadway, across from City Lights, 986-9651) which features leather booths, a signature coffee/liqueur drink, and bartenders from the set of *The Shining*. (There's a VIP back room for visiting celebrities like Sam Shepard, de Niro, whoever.)

Close by the pre-Beat Era legendary **Vesuvio's** bar (255 Columbus at Broadway, 362-3370, next to City Lights) has a few view tables on the top floor which are fun to sit at. The completely unpretentious yet strewn-with-dusty-vintage-artifacts **Spec's** bar (12 Saroyan Place, across from City Lights, 421-4112), is another North Beach bohemian landmark. If there's any place left where you can engage in lengthy political/anarchist discussions, Spec's would be it. You can take those rare radical tomes by Max Stirner or Karl Kraus you found at City Lights to Spec's and wave them about, and nobody will pay you the slightest attention.

Besides City Lights, probably the last concentrated bohemian hangout left in North Beach is **Caffe Trieste** (601 Vallejo at Grant, 392-6739) which still features a Saturday morning singalong of Italian classic songs, an opera-singing contest, and infinite indulgence of wannabe writers, radical philosophers, computer-geek-hacker-renegades and other malcontents (S.U.V.-driving yuppies also drop in for a quick coffee to go - the Trieste's coffee is second to none - but they really don't belong here). As far as coffeehouses go, I prefer sitting outdoors on all but the coldest and rainiest days, and near the Trieste the neighborhood sidewalk seller/artist/local character Fanny usually has an interesting display of "flea market" goods for sale, including her own paintings. The Trieste Annex next door offers my personal favorite coffee, Dark French Roast, ground to your specifications. This coffee is very dark, very oily and very aromatic: instant wakefulness is guaranteed

San Francisco's alpine-like **Julius' Castle** (1541 Montgomery, 648-1054), a landmark at least 50 years, sits perched like an eyrie at the dead end of Montgomery and Greenwich. It offers valet parking, so walk or take a bus there (the 39 Coit stops a block away). The food is expensive but in the afternoons the price of a drink buys a lot of ambience and an amazing, sweeping view. This is old San Francisco dining, like Dashiell Hammett must have enjoyed, with what they used to call Old World service.

While only offering bottled water and sodas (in the drinks department), **Coit Tower** (1 Telegraph Hill, 362-0808) is a deservedly famous San Francisco landmark. It's well worth the pricey admission to climb to the top and enjoy a 360-degree view of the entire Bay Area - almost. But beyond the gorgeous art deco design of the Coit Tower installation, it's the murals inside Coit Tower which continue to amaze and inspire wonder. San Francisco used to be a very radical place, a magnet for rebels from all over the globe, and the proof is in this 360-degree mural, which depicts the gamut of society from hard industry and farming to striking workers and "communist" books... the entire subtext of the painting can be neatly summed up in the phrase "class struggle." More than a mere work of art, this is visual history to inspire the Vladimir Lenins and Karl Marxes of tomorrow... or is it the Guy deBords and Raoul Vaneigems?

My favorite deli remains **Molinari** (373 Columbus at Vallejo, 421-2337), which gives free salami slices to small children, and has one of the widest selections of gourmet (yet not overpriced) food imports from Italy and elsewhere, including porcini mushrooms ($55/pound). Their sandwiches are legendary and huge, and their fresh pastas (spinach and white) at $1.50/lb. are just plain staples. In the refrigerator room they have homemade vegetarian tomato sauce (recommended), a Bolognese sauce and the best pesto this side of the **Caffe Sport** (574 Green at Columbus, 981-1251), an incredibly baroque naive art masterpiece of décor - lunch is fantastic and affordable, but dinner is not. This place deserves mini-museum status.

There are quite a number of good cafes in North Beach

- my favorite is the **Caffe Puccini** (411 Columbus at Vallejo, 989-7033) where I like to sit outside and watch passersby, but arguably the **Europa** (310 Columbus at Broadway, 391-5779) a few doors down has superior coffee and desserts. Still, Lawrence Ferlinghetti can be seen occasionally in both of these cafes in the mornings, reading an Italian newspaper and scribbling in a pad - don't disturb him! My favorite dessert can be found at the **Stella Pastry Cafe** (446 Columbus at Green, 986-2914) across the street: sacripantina (a cloud-like cake made with zabaglione cream and rum) and it is divine. The friendly staff will also decorate it for free on the spot ("Happy Birthday," etc.) This cake must be kept refrigerated and is best eaten soon after purchase; to the best of my knowledge never has there ever been any left over, anywhere. Supposedly this is a North Beach "exclusive" treat unavailable anywhere else on the planet. The other great Italian bakery, which has been here for decades, is **Victoria Pastry** (1362 Stockton at Vallejo, 781-2015). They make a traditional chocolately chocolate cake which they will also decorate/personalize on the spot.

My favorite neighborhood walk starts with espresso and pastry at an outdoor table at the French magazine store/cafe at Bush and Grant, across form the Chinatown gates. Snake your way through Chinatown, exploring every possible alley between Kearny and Stockton (which parallel Grant Avenue). Cross Broadway (until the '70s, the dividing line between Chinatown and the mostly-Italian North Beach), continue up Grant Avenue, turn right on Filbert and walk all the way to Coit Tower, saving time to explore the walkways on the harbor side of the slope around Julius's Castle. Retrace your steps down Union Street and turn left on where you will discover the still-enchanting Macondray Lane, the real-life setting for Armistead Maupin's novel *Tales of the City*. Upon reaching Leavenworth, turn left and circle back down the steep stairs on Green towards Powell. Go left on Powell, grab a sandwich at **Curly's** (1624 Powell at Green, 392-0144) and walk down Columbus Ave, turning left on Chestnut to the **S.F. Art Institute** (800 Chestnut at Jones, 771-7021). Admission is free and the roof has a panoramic view, plus a very cheap but delicious cafe. Don't miss the Diego Rivera mural. Continue down Columbus Ave (stopping at **Tower Records** at Columbus and Bay, 885-0500, for their free monthly magazine *Pulse*) toward Fisherman's Wharf, now glutted with glitzy tourist stores - by a miracle the **S.F. Wax Museum** (145 Jefferson, 202-0400) still remains. It's expensive, but the free tourist guides left at major hotels often contain discount coupons. In the basement is a replica of King Tut's tomb as well as deceased satanist Anton Lavey performing a satanic ritual. Disneylandish tourist sinkhole **Pier 39** has one saving grace: a free place to watch, smell and listen to the sea lions cavorting on large wooden floating platforms. Walk back along Grant Ave toward North Beach and at Filbert turn right, stopping at the **Liguria Bakery** (1700 Stockton at Filbert, 421-3786) for delicious cheap foccacia bread which you can eat at **Washington Square Park**, weather permitting. (If the adjacent St. Peter & Paul's Cathedral is open, it's worth a visit for the kitsch statuary and imposing gothic architecture.) There's a statue of Ben Franklin in the center of the park, and nearby a time capsule was buried by then-mayor Dianne Feinstein in 1977, containing (among other artifacts) a copy of my first punk publication, *Search & Destroy*.

A few other parks where one can linger and daydream include the little-known **Michelangelo Park** on Greenwich near Jones (catering to families and children; don't leave cigarette butts) and the much-more-grittily-urban Chinatown ethnic-theme **Portsmouth Square Park** off Washington between Kearny and Grant. One can also eat a bag lunch on the grass surrounding Coit Tower and reflect upon how architecture (and everything environmental, except California food and wine) has declined since the Art Deco period.

Travelers on a budget may stay at the **Green Tortoise** (490 Broadway at Kearny, 834-1000) or apply to the **Golden Eagle** (402 Broadway at Montgomery, 781-6859), the **St. Paul** (935 Kearny at Pacific, 986-9911), the **Europa** (310 Columbus at Broadway, 391-5779), the **Sestri** (1411 Stockton at Vallejo, 421-2734), and the small hotels facing Chinatown Park (Kearny at Clay), or try the youth hostel at idyllic **Fort Mason** (Building 240, Bay at Franklin, 771-7277). Besides downtown and the Tenderloin, pricier lodging may be found near Pacific and Van Ness - still within walking distance of North Beach - or in the Marina along Lombard St. There are tiny residence hotels throughout Chinatown and North Beach, but most are full.

Editor's Picks

The **U.S. Restaurant** (515 Columbus at Union, 397-5200) rules. The sandwiches on French bread are huge and accompanied by a pile of fries. Specials change daily, and on Friday nights, the red clam chowder and fried calamari are king. And the artichoke hearts sautéed in garlic are fantastic. For breakfast or brunch, the spinach omelet is superb, although it's more of a frittata than a typical omelet.

The Gold Spike (527 Columbus at Union, 421-4591) has a funky interior, and serves humongous, multicourse dinners for reasonable prices. The Friday night Crab Cioppino is highly recommended, and no one ever leaves hungry.

The Italian-French Baking Company (1501 Grant, 421-3796) at the corner of Grant and Union has incredible biscotti, as well as amazing hefty rosemary baguettes for 95 cents.

An amazingly surreal flock of **wild parrots**, green bodies with red near their beaks, live around Telegraph Hill and North Beach. In October, they are often seen in the pine trees at Washington Square Park, eating the nuts out of pinecones. They squawk loudly, and can often be heard flying overhead. And everyday between 8 and 9 a.m. in Washington Square Park, elderly Chinese people exercise and do tai chi en masse — truly an unusual sight to behold, if you're an early riser. Rumor has it that Marilyn Monroe and Joe DiMaggio got married in the big church facing the Park (DiMaggio grew up in North Beach), but they actually got married at City Hall.

Of historical interest, 1360 Montgomery, a cool art deco building, was where Lauren Bacall lived in the Bogart classic, *Dark Passage*. 1010 Montgomery Street is where Allen Ginsberg was living when he wrote *Howl*.

The currently-closed **Purple Onion** (140 Columbus) is where Phyllis Diller got her start, and Maya Angelou sang and danced there in the '50s (and you thought she was just a poet).

949 Lombard is the house where MTV's *Real World* San Francisco segment was filmed.

29 Russell (which is an alley between Hyde and Larkin, and Green and Union) was Neal Cassady's residence, where Jack Kerouac put the finishing touches on his novel *On The Road*.

The **Wave Organ** is a human-built, natural sound machine with incredible views of Golden Gate Bridge. Nearby, the **Presidio Pet Cemetery** is one of the more upscale places to end up as a dead dog. Marina Green is a good place to fly a kite. And nearby, the **Palace of Fine Arts** (Baker at Marina Blvd.) is a romantic place to have a picnic, but bring a sweater in case the fog rolls in.

THE RICHMOND, THE PARK, AND THE BEACH
BY MIRIAM WOLF

The Richmond District — or the "Upper West Side" as a friend refers to it because of its geographic location in the Northwest quadrant of San Francisco — is a neighborhood that doesn't get any respect. "Too suburban," the hipsters snort. "Always foggy."

Good. That just means its pleasures are more private.

The Richmond stretches 48 blocks, from Arguello to the ocean, from Lake Street to Fulton. It encompasses two of the more impressive parks in the U.S.: the **Presidio** (a former military base) and **Golden Gate Park**, plus a smaller patch of green, **Lincoln Park**. You can surf, swim, and sunbathe (in the buff at some locations) along the Richmond's well-kept urban beaches. It has touches of coffee house culture, as well as a varied immigrant population, with pockets of Russian, Asian, and Irish culture.

While the Richmond with its cookie-cutter stucco apartment buildings might seem drab compared to neighborhoods like North Beach, it does have one of the city's more fascinating attractions, one that's relaxing and sort of creepy at the same time: The **Neptune Society's Columbarium** (1 Loraine Ct., off Anza by Arguello, 771-0717). Housed in a beautiful four-story 1898 building, the Columbarium is a burial vault for cremated remains. Some famous San Francisco families have members in residence, including the Magnins (of department store fame) and the Folgers (think coffee). The niches are often decorated with icons that give a sense of the deceased's personality. One caveat here: go early, the Columbarium is open every day, but only from 10 a.m. to 1 p.m.

While you're in the inner Richmond, check out the absolute best of the city's bookstores (of course, I may be biased since I live four blocks away). **Green Apple Books** (506 Clement at 6th Ave., 387-2376) is a fab place to browse for books both new and used. As soon as you walk in the door, that musty, mouthwatering "bookstore aroma" hits your senses and you start figuring out what percentage of all the money on your person you want to spend here.

After visiting the deceased and spending a few hours inside a bookstore, you might want to get a little fresh air. **Golden Gate Park**, a few long blocks from Clement, is a green, accommodating oasis. Sunday is a great day for a park visit — the main road, JFK Drive, is closed to traffic, making it a haven for bikers and in-line skaters of all ages and proficiency levels (pedestrians: take extra care in crossing).

The Park is also where you'll find a couple of the city's more respected (read: mainstream) museums. Once a park gem, The **Asian Art Museum** (379-8800), boasting a fine collection of Japanese and Chinese works, is currently closed for relocation, but is set to re-open in early 2003 in the Civic Center. But still a long standing park fixture, the **California Academy of Science** (750-7145) is where you go to play. It features a sizable aquarium, a planetarium, and cool exhibits like the one where you can experience an earthquake. Nearby, the **Japanese Tea Garden** (9th Ave. at Lincoln, 668-0909) is peaceful and meditative, while the **Strybing Arboretum** (9th Ave. at Lincoln, 661-1316) and the **Conservatory of Flowers** will tell you all you've ever wanted to know about the greenery. Of course, museums aren't cheap anymore, and even the Tea Garden charges an entry fee, so the thing to remember here can be summed up in three words: Free First Wednesday. Yes, the first Wednesday of every month, all the museums in San Francisco throw open their doors to the public, and forget to charge admission. Yes it's crowded, but for most of us, it's worth it.

In the mood for a not-too-taxing hike? You can follow the **Coastal Trail** from the end of the Marina, up through to Fort Point (with a cool view of the big orange bridge), and down the coast until you hit the parking lot for the **Cliff House**. Warning: Bring your own food! Do not eat at the Cliff House, which is overpriced and has only passable food (though at night, the bar is a nice spot for an (again pricey) cocktail.

While you're in the area, poke around the former **Sutro Baths**. Now just a hole in the ground, the Baths used to be the place for San Franciscans to socialize in swimming suits. You can also check out the **Musee Mechanique** (1090 Point Lobos, 386-1170) a museum dedicated to coin-operated amusement, from vintage peep shows (hot-cha!) to children's games. The **Camera Obscura** is there, too — a kind of giant camera that you can walk inside for a virtual look at the sunset.

Ocean Beach, which stretches from the Cliff House to Fort Funston is where you can catch some sun (if you're lucky), wade in the waves, see surfers (wearing wetsuits, of course — the water is damn cold year round), and see a wide variety of city dwellers getting sand in their shoes. Even on the coolest days, you can find people there walking dogs, playing catch, or just strolling along the surf.

Wanna get naked? Scenic **North Baker Beach** is a traditional (if not strictly legal) nude beach that attracts its fair share of crowds on the weekends. It's accessible by a trail that starts near Ft. Point and winds its way down the beach. Remember, it's not nice to stare.

Worked up an appetite yet? The Richmond has some of the best inexpensive restaurants in the city. You can get a good meal in most of the following restaurants for less than $10.

Khan Toke Thai House (5937 Geary at 23rd Ave., 668-6654), with its pretty good eats and on-the-floor-take-off-your-shoes seating, is a good bet if your want a "dining experience," not just a meal.

While we're on the subject of theme dining, **El Mansour** (3123 Clement, 751-2312) is a moderately priced (read: not cheap) Moroccan restaurant, complete with belly dancers. Love the filo specialties.

Vietnamese? **Le Soleil** (133 Clement at 2nd Ave., 668-4848) has a delectable tofu with coconut milk dish that's rich and indulgent. **Taiwan Restaurant** (445 Clement at 6th Ave., 387-1789) has Taiwanese specialties on the menu, along with more familiar Chinese dishes. It's busy on weekend mornings, when the locals crowd in for dim sum.

The Richmond is an area full of bars, from the **Plough and Stars** (116 Clement, 751-1122) where Guinness is the drink of choice and traditional Irish music creates a good atmosphere for a game of darts, to **Pat O'Shea's Mad**

Hatter (5848 Geary, 752-3148), an always-crowded sports bar. But you'll need a proper base for your beer. That's where **Giorgio's** (151 Clement at 3rd Ave, 668-1266) comes in, with it's heavy but yummy calzones, stabilizing garlic bread, and massive salads.

Get wired for a day of shopping with a shot of espresso from one of the many cafes in the Richmond. There's the tiny, funky **Cool Beans** (4342 California at 6th. Ave, 750-1955); the cavernous hangout **Java Source** (343 Clement at 4th Ave, 387-8025) with its poetry readings every Tuesday night; and **I Love Chocolate** (397 Arguello at Clement, 750-9460), which has the best brownies in town.

BERKELEY
BY JONATHAN WATERS

All right, so you want to see Berkeley. You're going to need an outfit and a few essential accessories. For your dress, you must decide on the basic question of dressing up: do I want to be noticed or not? If you wish to be anonymous, some clean jeans with moderate flare, some earth shoes, brown, a roll-neck sweater, J. Crew perhaps, and if it's winter, if it's ever really winter in the Bay Area, some form of parka, green or any shade of ecological color. Basically that's the politically correct outfit. The coat could be red or bright yellow instead, implying you would be able to survive not only in town but in many of the base camps of Everest. With these garments, you could carry some thoughtful book like *The Snow Leopard* by Peter Matthieson, or *The Way of a Peaceful Warrior* by Dan Milman. You get the drift.

The other choice, the one I'm going to recommend,

consists of dark pants, some form of black top, be it dressy or a t-shirt, black sharp shoes and if it's cold, a leather jacket. The jacket is optional because it will identify you as one who wears animal skins, an identification which even I certainly don't crave but resent that any jacket makes me part of an offending class. Ah, well. With this outfit you will need three cigarettes (it doesn't matter if you smoke) and you could carry some more questionable tome, like Chet Baker's *Guide to Optimum Health*.

So let's say we start at the bottom of **University Avenue**. As you exit Highway 80, if you were willing to break six or seven traffic regulations, you could stop on the little bridge over the freeway and, like Caesar, survey the town you are about to conquer. It is basically, like many American communities, a square town. Starting from the verdant flats of **Cesar Chavez Marina Park** it rises slowly at first and then more sharply to the houses atop Grizzly Peak. To the North, its border is roughly **Solano Avenue**, a street known for inexorably slow drivers and family values. South is **Alcatraz Avenue**, a much faster throughway where many of the houses tilt a little as if part of a jazz melody. For all practical purposes, if you have a map, you should highlight Alcatraz, Dwight, and Marin avenues for your east-west motion, Sacramento and Hopkins for your north-south. Never go on Ashby. Shattuck can work but the downtown has more lights than a Christmas tree. Beware of little streets. Berkeley has erected more speed bumps and barricades than many towns actually under attack and consequently, even the fire trucks take a while to get somewhere.

Let's pretend it's morning. Do we want coffee? If you follow the dictum When in Rome... then you should start with caffeine, for there are eighty-seven establishments in Berkeley that solely want to sell you their black juice. If it's a regular cup of Joe you're after, the best is a tie between

Royal Coffee (307 63rd St. at College, Emeryville, 510-652-4256) and **Peet's** (2112 Vine at Walnut, 510-841-0564). Royal is a hang-out spot for the cool twenty-to-thirties with attitude but not much arrogance. This is the place where your black outfit would blend in fine. Order coffee as if you were weaned on some Arabian blend. Take a table outside. Watch the show, but don't stare. An insouciant but positive attitude would be best, as if all life bemused you and you are just pausing before you return home to finish your thesis on Paul Bowles.

Peet's coffees are all over town but the original one is on Walnut and Vine. There's a show here too, but it's more of a freak show, featuring people who have a different way of seeing the world and sometimes like to share it, loudly. Some of this might be attributed to the dark roast of Peet's coffee, which if you are not used to, could double your heartbeat. It's stronger than missile fuel and just as deadly. I would also recommend donning the leather jacket here to keep people away, but then again you might raise someone's ire. It's your call.

If you want an espresso beverage or any milky derivation thereof, the **French Hotel** (1538 Shattuck at Cedar, 510-548-9930) is a good choice, having taken the time to train their baristas. At the French Hotel, Angel has been making perfect cappuccinos for fourteen years, but there's nowhere very comfortable to sit. Take a table outside and wonder when do these people work? **Odyssia** () uses Illy beans, which are the best in the world, and offers more welcoming respite either on the street or inside its warm walls. They also serve various foods, including a hot bowl of semolina which one of my friends swears by for morning sustenance. Another option would be **Cafe Fanny** (1603 San Pablo Ave. at Cedar, 510-524-5447) which serves creamy cafe au laits in French bowls. You can get breakfast there too, but it will cost you a good chunk of change, so you might be better off trawling down to **Bette's-To-Go** (1807 4th at Hearst, 510-548-9494) on Fourth Street or **Rick & Anne's** (2922 Domingo Ave. at Ashby, 510-649-8538) up near the Claremont Hotel. Both serve an essential diner's breakfast, good quality, honest food, albeit a few dollars more than in Burlington, Vermont. Other breakfast spots would be **Saul's Deli** (1475 Shattuck at Vine, 510-848-3354) where they start you with a big bowl of pickles and mustard. Does that sound good? It is. Or if it's the weekend, **Picante Taqueria & Cantina** (1328 6th St. at Gilman, 510-525-3121) does a bang-up huevos rancheros and Mexican fare all day long.

Do you want to shop? Fourth Street has become the gathering place for traditional shoppers and certainly offers the chance of perusing the cool shoes at **Rabat** (1825 4th St. at Hearst, 510-549-9195) or listening to any CD you please at **Hear Music** (1809 4th at Hearst St., 510-204-9595). Across the street is **The Gardener** (1863 4th Street at Hearst, 510-548-4545) which gives one lots of hopes for how you wish your apartment could look rather than how it does. However, if this area starts to feel like an uncovered mall, then best wander up to Telegraph or College avenues. If a Mother's Day or wedding gift is required, the **Crate & Barrel Outlet** (1785 4th St., 510-528-5500) has pretty decent prices.

Telegraph Avenue offers one overcooked reduction of Berkeley's political past. Like the Haight, its present denizens are a motley collection of young down-and-outs and older eccentrics. On the weekends, the street is crammed with stalls in front of the stores, and if one wishes to experience the street life of Berkeley, there is no better place. You can purchase a three piece tie-dye outfit, have beads braided in your hair, and have your Tarot cards read, all in one block. Again, I would choose the black outfit and I would at least have a cigarette out, because you will be bothered less as a potential source of income, though nine or ten people might hit you up for that cigarette. **Mars** (2398 Telegraph at Channing, 510-843-6711) sells used clothes and costumes at the corner of Channing Way. **Moe's Books** (2476 Telegraph at Dwight, 510-849-2087) has floors of used and new books at extremely reasonable prices. There are also varied hip-hop clothing stores up and down the street, for one's enjoyment.

College Avenue reaches its best shopping around Ashby Avenue. For clothes, both **Jeremy's** (2967 College Ave. at Ashby, 510-849-0701) and **Dish** (2981 College Ave. at Ashby, 510-540-4784) are worth a visit. Jeremy's sells more conventional clothes and re-sold seconds at slash-down prices. Be careful, however "as-is" can mean trouble with some of the garments. Dish, just south of Jeremy's, plies a cooler collection of men's and women's clothes, and the owner Desiree is just as wonderful as her clothes. Half a block south on Ashby is the store **Tail of the Yak Trading Co.** (2632 Ashby Ave. at College, 510-841-9891), which has a great collection of Mexican art and ribbons. It may sound strange but for the little house present it never lets one down.

Next: Lunch. If you want a sandwich and are on the south side of Berkeley, **Genova Delicatessen & Ravioli Factory** (51st at Telegraph, 510-652-7401), technically in Oakland (well, it is in Oakland) has the best sandwiches in town. Grab a number, grab a roll and be ready to tell them what you want. They don't waste time nor your money and you're sated for under a fiver. One last suggestion for lunch would be **Cheeseboard Pizza** (1512 Shattuck at Vine, 510-549-3183) up on Shattuck. Like most of the gourmet ghetto, there's not many places to sit, but the food is superb. **The**

Cheeseboard (1504 Shattuck, 510-549-3183) sells wonderful rolls - their oatmeal scone is one of the five foods I'd take with me to a desert island, more cheeses than Wisconsin and a superb slice of pizza for a buck and a half. For dinner on the cheaper side, Cheeseboard can also sell you a half-baked pizza which you can bring home to please your friends.

Across the street is **Chez Panisse** (1517 Shattuck at Cedar, 510-548-5525 for dinner, or 510-548-5049 for the cafe) which is going to cost significantly more but be every bit as delicious and will offer you a comfortable seat. Or down the block is **Cha-Am** (1543 Shattuck at Cedar, 510-848-9664) an always busy Thai restaurant serving food on the sweet and spicy side. If you missed Vic's for lunch, another Indian establishment for supper is **Breads of India** (2448 Sacramento at Dwight, 510-848-7684). Their daily changing menu is extremely tasty and not expensive. Queue for a table and pick some bread you've never heard of to go with your curry. If you are with a bunch of friends and no one agrees, you could cross borders down to the **Emeryville Market** (starts at 5959 Shellmound, 510-652-9300), where about twenty vendors sell anything from fettucine Alfredo to Korean bim-bi-baob. If you want Mexican, I'd return to **Picante's** (1328 6th St. at Gilman, 510-525-3121) and order their Sopa di Pollo, a soup so delicious it will cure almost any ailment.

Past supper, Berkeley does start to slow down for many of its inhabitants. For after-dinner drinks and to mingle with the most stylish, **Cesar's** (1515 Shattuck at Cedar, 510-883-0222), next to Chez Panisse, would be our choice. Definitely wear black, make it look like you're about to smoke any second, and if you're adventurous, let Kathleen the bartendress choose your poison. The alcohol selection here is encyclopedic, and if you have the constitution for it, and the wallet, you can go a long way here. On the cheaper side of drinks, the **Albatross Pub** (1822 San Pablo Ave. at University, 510-843-2473) is the closest thing to an English pub Berkeley has to offer. Great beer selection, darts, a fireplace, unlimited free popcorn and a scene friendly to all. In case this hasn't worked, you're still hungry, and it's past midnight, don't let anyone tell you you're out of luck. **The Smokehouse** (3115 Telegraph Ave. at Woolsey, 510-845-3640) serves steaming hot burgers (vegetarian as well) and fries to the wee hours. You can sit outside, smoke, or again just hold, your last cigarette and relax in the fact that although Berkeley hasn't changed much of your political outlook, it has at least assuaged your gastronomic needs.

Editor's Picks

Berkeley Bowl (2020 Oregon at Shattuck, 510-843-6929) Organic food shopping central; fabulous produce and more.

Berkeley Farmers Market (Center & MLK Jr Way, 510-548-6929) Saturdays: it's all good. Don't miss it.

Grocery Outlet (2000 5th St. near University, 510-845-1999) aka The Museum of Lost Food. Godlike grocery store for bargain hunters. Keep an open mind and don't go with an agenda.

Berkeley Flea Market (Ashby BART parking lot, Ashby & MLK Jr Way) Saturdays and Sundays. You never know what'll turn up here. Good people-watching and fun perusals.

Tilden Park (Wildcat Canyon Rd. & Grizzly Peak Blvd., 510-562-PARK) Go for a swim in Lake Anza, play golf, ride the vintage carousel and the best miniature steam train in the Bay Area. Lots of scenic hiking trails and more.

UC Berkeley's **Greek Theater** Built in 1903, this outdoor concert venue is one of the greatest in the Bay Area.

BERKELEY

On a clear day, you can see the entire bay and beyond from the top of the lawn. Highly recommended.

UNEXPECTED OAKLAND
BY DASHKA SLATER

Oakland is a city of pockets, of unexpected things. It takes a while to get to know it and a lifetime to understand it, but those of us who live here love it the way poets love poetry. We know the rest of the world considers us irrelevant, but we think we've found the key to everything.

If San Francisco is an international city, Oakland is an American one, as quixotic and perplexing as America itself. Oakland is America as it used to be: a city of railroads and shipyards. Oakland is America as it will be: neither white, nor black, nor Asian nor Latino nor Native American, but all of these together. It has sun in summer, 22 miles of shoreline, a redwood forest and a saltwater lake but it doesn't wear its attributes on its sleeve. Even now that it has a famous former governor as its mayor, and a steady stream of San Franciscans relocating to its cheaper and sunnier shores,

Oakland is still a bit secretive about its treasures. When you set out to visit Oakland, you have to be a sleuth, because this is a city of hidden things, of dusty shops and secret passageways. Here are some clues as to what to look for, but the best things are the ones you find on your own.

BOOKSTORES

The Bay Area is filled with wonderful, well-stocked independent bookstores and Oakland is no exception. But the city also has an unparalleled selection of antiquarian bookshops, places filled with dusty treasures and strange serendipitous wonders, first editions, collections of ancient books on flying saucers and military history, and they are all scattered in and around downtown. Here you can find **Bibliomania** (1816 Telegraph Ave. at 19th, 510 835-5733) which specializes in books on social movements with things like anti-lynching tracts from the pre-civil rights era South, the collected works of Mussolini, in Italian, and a startling selection of books and pamphlets about flying saucers and other occultist movements. Down the street is **My Book Heaven** (2212 Broadway at 22nd, 510 893-7273), heaven in this case being a store full of novels and children's books, all of which are first editions. A few blocks away is **Dan Webb Books**, with its extensive collection of military histories and regional American cookbooks (15 Grand Ave. at Broadway, 510-444-4572).

Smack in the middle of downtown is **De Lauer Super Newsstand** (1310 Broadway at 13th, 510 451-6157) which has an enormous selection of magazines and newspapers from all over the world and has the added advantage of being open 24 hours a day. Over in Old Oakland is the **Friends of the Oakland Public Library** store (721 Washington at 7th and 8th, 510 444-0473), with its ever changing collection of plastic-covered discards. This is a great place to find old children's books and tawdry romance novels. Veering even farther from the world of literature is the **Western Christian Bookstore** (1618 Franklin at 17th, 510 832-2040), a place which carries underground comics far more depraved than Horny Biker Sluts, for only twelve cents each. I'm speaking of the pocket sized comic book tracts from Chick Publications that explain how Halloween is a cover for Satanists who want to murder little children, how the Catholic Church is conspiring to bring communism and Mary worship to the world, and other little known facts. Just don't giggle too loudly while you're in the store, or they'll boot you out.

ART

With its big empty warehouses and low rents, Oakland is a perfect haven for artists, and it is rumored to have more artists in residence than just about any city in the country, with the exception of New York. It is also the place to get a feel for what California art is about, as opposed to that washed-out, bloodless stuff they import from New York and put in the SFMOMA. **The Oakland Museum** (1000 Oak St. at Tenth, 510-238-2200) is the official Museum of California, containing the best and most extensive collection of California art from the age of exploration to the present. There are also history and a natural science departments. Between the three divisions there is always at least one outstanding special exhibition, and the permanent collections are well worth gawking at in and of themselves. Make sure to go through the little screen door in the main art gallery to see the miniature SoCal valley scene, complete with trailer, dump site and freeway noise. A few blocks away, the **Oakland Museum's Sculpture Garden** (1111 Broadway, 510 238-2200) is in the lobby of the American President Lines Building and has small, innovative sculpture exhibits in a sunny atrium gallery.

Pro Arts Gallery in Old Oakland (461 Ninth St. at Broadway, 510-763-4361, www.proartsgallery.org) is the foremost gallery in the East Bay, with a different exhibit every month and a great gallery shop at the front. They also sponsor the East Bay open studio exhibit every June. The **Ebony Museum of Art** (30 Jack London Village at Embarcadero, Suites 208-209, 510 763-0141) showcases African and African American art and artifacts, from 1960s issues of Ebony magazine to intricately beaded figures from Zaire and Cameroon. Most amazing of all is Aissatoui A. Vernita's spooky and beautiful soul food sculptures - a bench made out of beef shoulder blade bones, a church made of fatback, mustard and collard greens, and beef and chicken bones. In the same building is Samuel's Gallery which carries prints, limited editions and originals by more than 250 black and African artists like William Toliver, Ernie Barnes and Synthia Saint James. One of the best, and most unusual, places to see art is **Creative Arts Gallery** (355 24th St. at Broadway, 510-836-2340) which shows the work of "outsider" artists - artists with emotional or mental disabilities. The work is amazing - emotional, exuberant, humorous and utterly unlike anything you'll see anywhere else. Across the street from Jack London Square is the **Museum of Children's Art** (9th St. at Clay, 510-465-8770), better known as MOCHA. The artists on display range from very young to high school age, but the art is always surprising - and often less childish than much of the stuff you see in the adult galleries. Mocha is also a great place to bring kids for hands-on art projects.

For more information on Oakland arts, check out the City of Oakland's web page at www.oaklandnet.com/arts. It's also worth calling the **Artship Foundation** (510-272-4879) to see whether they're offering tours of the ArtShip, a former World War II troop carrier that's being converted into a floating artspace, with galleries, theaters, cafes, and a maritime museum.

SITES, ATTRACTIONS & WALKS

The best way to get a feel for Oakland is to wander through its neighborhoods, which are doing their best to retain their native character, despite incursions from Starbucks, the Gap, and other chains. You can walk the length of East Fourteenth Street, to get a feel for all the nationalities that make up this very multi-cultural city, or browse through the boutiques and cafes of the more upscale The Rockridge/ College Avenue neighborhood. You might amble through Chinatown (more on that later), climb the 135 steps that make up the Cleveland Cascade (an extension of Cleveland Street near Lake Merritt). If you enjoy fantasizing about how you would live if you had piles of money, the Trestle Glen neighborhood (just off of Lake Shore Avenue) has acres of windy streets and houses built to resemble Tudor manses, Swiss chalets, antebellum mansions, and storybook castles. The 1920's-era neighborhood was designed by famed landscape architect Frederick Law Olmstead, the designer of New York's Central Park.

Olmstead also designed **Mountain View Cemetery** (5000 Piedmont at Pleasant Valley), which is in itself one of Oakland's most beautiful places to walk. The 220-acre cemetery is filled with winding paths, flowering trees, surprising little lakes, and wondrous monuments to the self-important dearly departed, giving proof to Ambrose Bierce's definition of mausoleum as "the final and funniest folly of the rich." The dead don't seem to mind that their final resting place is usually filled with joggers and bicyclists as well as mourners, so pack yourself a picnic lunch, set yourself down on the front stoop of the Crocker monument and enjoy the glorious view of the Bay. It's the kind of view that makes you glad to be alive. (For your picnic provisions, I suggest stopping at nearby **AG Ferrari Foods**, 2905 College Ave. at Ashby, 510-849-2701)

Olmstead designed the cemetery in the tradition of the "garden cemeteries" of the east, but used plants like Italian cypresses and Lebanese cedars that were suited to the aridity of the west. The cemetery quickly became the East Bay's poshest final resting place, attracting the mortal remains of such luminaries as architects Julia Morgan (who designed the beautiful Chapel of the Chimes next door) and Bernard Maybeck, industrialist Henry J. Kaiser, Emeryville founder Joseph Emery, chocolatier Domingo Ghirardelli, Chabot observatory founder Anthony Chabot, and Key System founder and washing products czar Francis "Borax" Smith. Perhaps the most egomaniacal of the notables interred there is temperance leader Henry David Cogswell, who had a 70-foot high granite obelisk erected over his tomb. The granite had to be brought from the East coast and at 329 tons was the heaviest shipment ever made at one time across the continent. It took 38 freight cars to carry it.

On the other end of the spectrum, **Evergreen Cemetery** (6450 Camden at 64th Ave.), is the final resting place for the remains of more than 400 unidentified members of the People's Temple, killed in the 1978 Jonestown massacre in Guyana. A simple marker shows where they are buried.

The most famous walk in Oakland is the 3.5 mile walk around Lake Merritt, and for good reason. The Lake is the best place to get a feel for Oakland as a truly multicultural city and if you are the kind of person who gets pleasure from just seeing all the different shades and shapes and styles human beings come in, this is the place to do it. The Lake used to be a tidal swamp before it was made into a saltwater lake and on hot, still days it can sometimes get a bit odiferous. Still, the scenery's pretty, and you can rent sailboats, paddleboats, kayaks, canoes and rowboats at the **Lake Merritt Boating Center** (568 Bellevue Ave. in Lakeside Park, 510-444-3807). Or, if you feel like touring the lake in style, you can recline in a genuine Venetian gondola and be serenaded by a gondolier. The gondolas are rented by Gondola Servizio, cost $55 for two (or $95 for a romantic sixsome), and include blankets and candlelight in the evening. You can bring your own wine and picnic, and they provide the glassware (for reservations call 510-663-6603, www.gondolaservizio.com).

If you have a kid with you, you can get into **Children's Fairyland**, (on the northern side of Lake Merritt at Grand Ave. and Bellevue, 510-238-6876) a decidedly surreal 1950s-era collection of painted storybook sculptures that speak with strange disembodied voices once you present them with a magic key. Not to be missed, but they won't let you in without a kid in tow.

Keep your eye out for the low-lying labyrinth on the edge of the Lake; it looks kind of like a strangely symmetrical collection of rodent burrows. This isn't the kind of labyrinth you get lost in, it's more of a spiritual journey, for those who don't have time for longer pilgrimages. Walking through the pattern is supposed to be a form of meditation, so tell your traveling companions to stop blathering and see if you get hit by any blinding insights while you're walking.

A similar maze can be found in **Sibley Volcanic Regional Preserve**, on Skyline Boulevard just south of the intersection with Grizzly Peak Boulevard, but you have to look for it. On a clear day you can see Mt. Diablo from here, and in spring there are wildflowers tucked among the ancient lava flows. Just south of the entrance to Sibley is **Huckleberry Botanic Regional Preserve**, a 132 acre self-guided nature trail where you can see a variety of rare native plants, including what the park district describes romantically as "elfin forests" of manzanita. Nearby, is **Redwood Regional Park**, the most popular of Oakland's wild parks because of its 150 foot redwoods and woodsy paths and gorgeous views. Take Stream Trail to see redwoods, East Ridge trail for vistas.

Some more fabulous walks can be taken at **Joaquin Miller Park**, which connects to the southern side of Redwood Park. Named for the "Poet of the Sierra" who once lived in these hills, the park not only has some lovely trails, but also boasts some peculiar poetical monuments constructed by Miller himself. Frequently costumed in buckskins and buffalo robes, Miller portrayed himself as a kind of archetypal Westerner at a time when the world was mad for such things. Before coming to Oakland, he panned for gold, took an arrow in the head during a battle between Mt. Shasta settlers and Modoc Indians, rode for the Pony Express, was nearly hanged as a horse thief, and then (turnabout being fair play) was elected judge of Canyon City, Oregon. In Oakland he lived at an estate he called "The Heights." There he palled around with other local wits — Jack London and Ambrose Bierce among them — and wrote a lot of pretty awful poetry. (A sample, from "In San Francisco": Yea, here sit we by the golden gate/Not demanding much, but inviting you all/Nor publishing loud, but daring to wait/And great in much that the days deem small;/And the gate it is God's, to Cathay, Japan,— /And who shall shut it in the face of man?)

Among the interesting things to be found in Joaquin Miller Park are the funeral pyre Miller built for himself, and the monument he constructed to Robert Barrett Browning. Both can be found along Sanborn Drive. To get there, take the Joaquin Miller Road exit from Highway 13 and take Joaquin Miller Road east, toward the hills. You'll see the entrance to the park on your left. At the ranger's station by the entrance (3590 Sanborn Drive at Joaquin Miller St., 510-482-7888) you can get a map of the park that points the way to the various sights, including both the funeral pyre, the Browning monument, and the remains of Miller's former house, The Heights." But don't stop there. Take a stroll into the park's leafy interior, filled with redwoods, manzanita, and live oaks. Some of the best trails are Sinawik, Sunset, and Sequoia Bay View.

Oakland's most notable literary figure is, of course, Jack London, whom many Europeans consider to be this country's most accomplished writer. London memorabilia is clustered in and around Jack London Square, so named because a youthful London used to hang around the Oakland wharves. You can view first editions of some of his 52 books at the **Jack London Museum** (30 Jack London Square at Embarcadero), and there are even a few cheesecake shots of a bare-bummed Jack, taken for his medical records. Jack London Square also retains the writer's favorite bar, **Heinhold's First and Last Chance Saloon** (56 Jack London Square at Embarcadero, 510-839-6761). A tiny little shed with more than a hundred years build up of cigarette smoke and stale beer smell, the saloon is still lit by gas lanterns and has a slanted floor brought about by the 1906 earthquake.

Heinhold's is the last vestige of the old, funky Oakland waterfront, which has since been gussied up quite a bit and plastered with the kind of expensive, uninteresting restaurants and stores that plague waterfront developments worldwide. But there's still something appealing about Jack London Square. The view of the estuary is like something out of a painting, and the fancy restaurants can't conceal the fact that Oakland is still a working port, with trains, and tugboats, and giant cranes.

The best time to come to Jack London Square is during the Sunday morning farmers market or the Saturday afternoon **Antiques and Collectibles Market** (12-4 p.m., 510-814-6000), when the whole place has a festival atmosphere. But anytime that the weather is fine, Jack London Square is a great place to sit and watch the water. At the Roosevelt pier at the end of Clay Street there's a little observation tower where you can sit and have yourself a picnic and watch the sun sparkling on the estuary, the cranes unloading the container ships, and the progress of an assortment of vessels ranging from kayak to tanker.

Oakland's waterfront goes on for 22 miles, and if you know how to kayak you can rent a single or a double here at **California Canoe and Kayak** (409 Water at Franklin, 510 893-7833, $15 for singles, $20 for doubles) and tour the estuary yourself. The estuary is a wild place that includes a bizarre settlement of maritime gypsies and various other wonders, both natural and manmade - rusting barges and dilapidated warehouses, the race course for the Cal crew team, and a succession of drawbridges among them. If paddling isn't your bag, you can also tour the estuary aboard the Potomac, which was FDR's personal yacht once upon a time, or for $5 take a water taxi tour.

One thing you should not do in Jack London Square, if you can possibly help it, is eat. Most of the food nearby is overpriced and awful. Passable meals can be obtained at **Italian Colors** (101 Broadway at Park Blvd., 510-482-8094) or **Hahn's Hibachi** (63 Jack London Square, 510-628-0718), and the sushi at **Yoshi's** (510 Embarcadero West at Washington, 510- 238-9200) is good, but pricey. Better quality nosh for your nickel can obtained a few blocks away at the **Cuckoo's Nest** (247 Fourth St. at Alice, 510-452-9414) where you can get sandwiches, polenta, espresso and a good selection of wine and beer in a gorgeous warehouse café.

For a more contemporary take on Oakland history, sign up for the Black Panther Legacy Tour, sponsored by the Huey P. Newton Foundation and usually hosted by former Panther Party Chair David Hilliard. The two and a half hour tour leaves from the **West Oakland Library** (1801 Adeline Street) every Saturday at noon and takes you to eighteen sites of revolutionary activity. The cost is $20, reservations can be made at 510 986-0660.

Old Oakland and Chinatown are two neighborhoods right next to each other, in the area between 7th and 10th Streets. Old Oakland is on the west side of Broadway, Chinatown is on the east side, but both are great neighborhoods for just walking and exploring, either on your own or with a group. If you want a guide, call 510-238-3234 or 510-763-9218 to find out about the free walking tours that lead visitors through seven routes from May to October. Don't blanch at the word "tour" - these ones are very low key, and it's a good way to find some of the hidden spots - the beef jerky factory in Chinatown, for instance.

Chinatown is as much Southeast Asian as Chinese now, and unlike San Francisco's Grant Avenue it still functions as a residential neighborhood more than a tourist attraction. Here you'll find everything from a Hello Kitty store to shops selling gnarled roots and powdery herbs, and ones selling silk dresses, plastic toys and handmade paper. Recommended restaurants include **Vi's** for Vietnamese (724 Webster at 7th and 8th, 510-835-8375), and **Phnom Penh House** for Cambodian (251 8th St. at Alice, 510-893-3825). For Chinese food, check out **Shan Dong** (10th St. at Harrison, 510-839-2299, 510-893-3825) for delicious dumplings, and **Best Taste** (814 Franklin at 8th St., 510-444-4983) for roast meats. For Dim Sum, try the **Peony**

Restaurant (388 9th St. at Franklin, 510-286-8866) or **Tin's Teahouse** (701 Webster St. at 7th St., 510-832-7661).

If you prefer American or European cuisine, cross over to the Victorian-era streets and buildings of Old Oakland. At **Ratto's** (841 Washington at 9th, 510-832-6503) Italian deli you can get a sandwich to go, or during lunchtime hours you can hang out in the airy, high ceilinged dining room and make your selection from the cafeteria menu of pasta and gourmet sandwiches. A few doors down is **Caffe 817** (817 Washington at 9th, 510-271-7965) where you can get sandwiches, pastries and coffee, and if you're lucky enough to get an outdoor table, enjoy the sun. More outdoor tables are across the street at the **Pacific Coast Brewery** (906 Washington at 9th, 510-836-2739), which not only has a sunny beer garden and some of the best microbrewed beers in the nation, but it even has palatable pub food.

NIGHTLIFE PERFORMANCES

If the idea of slurping noodles while a burly tenor is doing a Pavarotti imitation next to your table appeals to you, go to **Ratto's** (821 Washington at 9th, 510-832-6503) on a Friday or Saturday night for their Pasta and Opera night. For $22.50 you get a four course dinner and the pleasure of hearing opera singers belt out arias and even a few show tunes. Some take requests. The evening starts at 6:30; reservations are highly recommended: 510 832-6503

Chabot Observatory (10902 Skyline Boulevard, 510-530-3480, www.cosc.org) is a brand new facility (opening in the summer of 2000) that features the largest public telescope in the U.S. It also has a 250-seat planetarium, and a 210-seat large-screen domed Megamax Science Theater, a "Challenger Learning Center" for space flight simulation, and other cool stuff.

At this writing, it's not clear yet what-all they're going

to be offering in the way of public programs, but they will certainly continue to let people come look through the telescopes on Friday and Saturday nights, with astronomers on hand to tell you what the hell it is you're looking at.

Built in 1926 and lovingly restored and expanded in the early '80s, **The Grand Lake Theater** (3200 Grand Ave. at MacArthur Blvd, 510-452-3556) is one of the best places in the world to see a first run movie It has electric fireworks exploding on its roof, faux marble pillars in its lobbies and Wurlitzer organ performances in the main theater before the show.

The best place to see an old movie is undoubtedly the **Paramount Theater** (2025 Broadway at 21st St., 510-465-6400), a theater that is even more lavish than the Grand Lake. Like the Grand Lake, the Paramount is an elegant old movie palace, with an immense elegant lobby, a glittering ceiling and a thousand other details that make you want to put on a satin evening gown and wear your hair like Veronica Lake. On selected Friday nights, the Paramount shows old movies complete with a short and a news reel, and even offers door prizes. The theater also has live performances by the Oakland Ballet and the Oakland East Bay Symphony, as well as various country, soul and gospel acts. To find out what's playing, call 510-465-6400.

Another great performing arts venue is the **Alice Arts Center** (1428 Alice at 14th St.), home of Dimensions Dance Theater and CitiCenter Dance Theater, the Oakland Ballet and the Oakland Ensemble Theater. Performances here are intermittent, but you can almost always take a dance class in one of the gorgeous old-fashioned dance studios - jazz, Haitian, Afro-Cuban, modern, ballet, salsa, hip-hop, flamenco, or samba. Call 510-238-7219 to find out about performances and dance classes.

BARS AND NIGHTCLUBS

Oakland was once the headquarters of the West Coast Blues, but there are only a few remnants of the old blues scene left. The most famous of these is **Eli's Mile High Club** (3629 Martin Luther King Jr. Way at 37th St., 510-655-6661), a crowded, lively little bar that always has live music. For jazz, the best quality is always at **Yoshi's** (510 Embarcadero West at Washington; 510-238-9200), probably the world's only Japanese restaurant and jazz club. This is where the top jazz acts in the nation come to play, but the cover prices are steep so be prepared. The best place to hear some form of hyphenated alternative sound (rock-pop-punk-funk-blues-trance-cabaret-folk) is the **Stork Club** in downtown Oakland, a hole-in-the-wall with year-round Christmas decor and a steady parade of cool bands (2330 Telegraph Ave. at 23rd St., 510-444-6174).

For other entertainment listings, check out the East Bay Express, the East Bay's free weekly newspaper (www.eastbayexpress.com).

But Oakland isn't as much of a nightclub town as it is a town full of peculiar little bars that are sort of elegant and sort of divey and all in all seem to be not quite of this decade. I like the Terrace Lounge at the swank **Claremont Hotel** (Ashby at Domingo Ave., 510-843-3000) because it has orange-hued fifties decor, a beautiful view of the Bay, and sometimes a decent jazz or swing band. Down a peg or two is the **Serenader** (504 Lake Park Ave. at Lake Shore, near the Grand Lake Theater, 510-832-2644). Having been a speakeasy, jazz club and private home, this oddball bar has seen just about everything you can imagine, which probably accounts for the attitude of geniality. Some nights there's a blues band, some nights not, but the mood is always kind of hip. Further down toward the dive end of the spectrum is **The Alley** (3325 Grand, 510-444-8505), a hole-in-the-wall bar that's decorated like a cartoon alley, the kind where humpbacked cats yowl on fence tops and pawnshop windows advertise "Money to Loan." The bar's focal point is a large piano topped with a ring of microphones where would-be crooners gather to warble Walking After Midnight and New York, New York. House pianist Rod Dibble's style of play can only be described as plinking and most of the singers are in that middle stage of inebriation where they can remember the words but can't carry a tune - but hey, if you think you can do better, pull up a mike and sing it yourself.

When morning comes, as it inevitably does, **Mama's Royal Café** (4012 Broadway at 40th St., 510-547-7600) is the best place to go to blast the hangover away with strong coffee and kick-ass omelets. This restaurant has the most awesome selection of breakfast delicacies, the coolest waitresses, along with a mounted collection of old aprons and radios and an ever-changing display of Napkin Art. There is always a wait on weekends, so bring the newspaper.

Index

Community Services

Dating

Education

Farmers Markets

Festivals & Parades

Food Stores

Gay & Lesbian
Eating Out

Radio Stations

Record Stores

Sex